Design in the
Age of Change

T0079905

Design in the Age of Change

Gjoko Muratovski

Bristol, UK / Chicago, USA

First published in the UK in 2022 by
Intellect, The Mill, Parnall Road, Fishponds, Bristol, BS16 3JG, UK

First published in the USA in 2022 by
Intellect, The University of Chicago Press, 1427 E. 60th Street, Chicago,
IL 60637, USA

A catalogue record for this book is available from the British Library.

Copy editor: MPS Limited
Cover designer: Gjoko Muratovski and Aleksandra Szumlas
Production manager: Laura Christopher
Typesetting: MPS Limited

Print ISBN 978-1-78938-545-8
ePDF ISBN 978-1-78938-546-5
ePUB ISBN 978-1-78938-547-2

Printed and bound by Short Run.

To find out about all our publications, please visit

www.intellectbooks.com.

There, you can subscribe to our e-newsletter,
browse or download our current catalogue,
and buy any titles that are in print.

Contents

Time capsule

Foreword by Srini R. Srinivasan
President, World Design Organization

It was January 2020 and the world was getting ready to have another great year. But instead, the year started with news about a new coronavirus disease called COVID-19. The virus, which originally started in Wuhan, China, began spreading quickly across the world, and the death toll started mounting. Italy and Spain were very badly affected in the first wave of the epidemic. Then, the virus quickly spread around the world. By March, the World Health Organization declared COVID-19 as a pandemic. This announcement caused panic across the globe and countries initiated lockdowns, travel bans, stay-at-home orders, and closure of borders.

Fear, anxiety, frustration, despair, and lack of reliable information were the initial reactions to this pandemic. Hundreds of thousands of people died, and millions more were infected. Health authorities were completely unprepared for this colossal attack on humanity. The continued dominance of COVID-19 brought even more damage on our society and on the global economy. Widespread poverty, joblessness, loss of businesses, and ever-present fear of getting infected or dying led to more frustration and despair. As if all this was not enough, soon after we saw political unrests, social, and racial justice movements such as Black Lives Matter, and other political events related to climate change, and so on. As I am writing this, all of the unfortunate events that defined 2020 are still fresh in my mind, and in the minds of everyone on the planet.

As all these challenges continued into 2021, the world has learned to adjust to new ways of living in every aspect of our lives. We embraced new personal habits, different kinds of work schedules, new forms of entertainment, spending more time indoors, learning new skills, we established new forms of communication with business, extended family, and friends, and, in some ways, we even kept our sense of humor intact.

In the midst of it all, Gjoko Muratovski managed to capture the spirit of these unsettling times by engaging in vivid conversation with a broad range of leading design figures today. Through these conversations, in a very engaging way, Gjoko draws on the personal opinions and experiences of people who come from various cultural, racial, geographical, and economic backgrounds. He begins this book, and his conversations, by referring to the "new normal"—a commonly embraced phrase today that encapsulates our current way of life during these times of change. Very successfully, Gjoko keeps the interest of the reader alive throughout this book.

The book, which is quite appropriately titled as *Design in the Age of Change*, examines the ever-changing state of design—from the past to the present, while looking into the future. This book is essentially a time capsule of what

Time capsule

the year 2020 was all about, and how we all come to accept the inevitable, adapt ourselves, and start preparing for a new future. By bringing together highly diverse designers that are leaders in their own domains, Gjoko has done an excellent job in representing the power of design during times of change.

This is a worthy read and a good addition to any book collection.

Acknowledgments

The development of the *Design in the Age of Change* book was based on the global speaker series called The New Normal, which was hosted by myself as the Director of The Myron E. Ullman, Jr School of Design at the time. The conversations that are featured in this book were conducted virtually, in a videoconference format. All of the interviews were recorded, transcribed, edited, and condensed for brevity and clarity. Every effort has been made to preserve the original intention behind the subject matter of the interview. This project included multiple participants and a large number of support staff. With this in mind, I would like to thank everyone who participated in these interviews and acknowledge the many people who helped me produce the speaker series on which this book is based.

First of all, I would like to thank Carole Bilson, Karim Rashid, Natalie Nixon, Bruce Mau, Steven Heller, Alok Vaid-Menon, Randall Wilson, Don Norman, Ida Telalbasic, and Mark Boudreaux for sharing their insights, perspectives, and personal experiences with me. Producing this project was a major effort. I would also like to thank all the unsung heroes who made all of this possible. My sincere thanks go to Sarah Chase, Dan Dugan, Jessica Gates, Sophia Tibbs, and Michael Everett for all their assistance with the production of the series, the video production, the copy editing, and the production of the associated collateral. I especially would like to thank my wife, Ekaterina Loy, for giving me the idea to develop this series while we were in lockdown due to, and for her help in conducting the background research.

I would also like to thank Tina Rayyan, Olga McConnell, Jessica Pearson, Judy Boudreaux, and Rhiya for all their help with making the arrangements behind some of these talks. My special thanks go to Srini R. Srinivasan, the President of the World Design Organization, for his encouragement and support, and for writing the foreword for this book, and to Ken Friedman for writing the afterword. In addition to this, I would like to thank everyone who participated in this overarching speaker series, such as Lisa Scharoun, Ashley Kubley, Melanie Finger, Ivana Zhiljak-Stanimirovic, Tamsin Greulich-Smith, Darryn Keiller, and Kylie Horomia.

This speaker series and book have been made possible with a financial support from The Myron E. Ullman, Jr Endowment Fund that I had the privilege to manage and facilitate on behalf of the Ullman School of Design and the Ullman Family. I also appreciate the support from the College of Design, Architecture, Art & Planning (DAAP)

Acknowledgments

at the University of Cincinnati. A special thanks goes to James Campbell, Tim Mitchell, and Laura Christopher from Intellect Books for commissioning and producing this book.

Welcome to "The New Normal"

Introduction by Gjoko Muratovski

In 2020, the world entered into a state of flux and social transformation. We reached a point in time when the world as we know it is undergoing a level of change beyond anything else that we have experienced in our lifetime. As a society, we have now reached the point of no return. Right now, as I am writing this introduction, we still don't know exactly where we are headed, nor how this change will look like once everything settles.

There is no doubt in my mind that 2020 will be a year that will remain in our collective memory. The world today is both terrifying and exciting place to be in. The COVID-19 pandemic, social inequality, racial injustice, climate change, gender issues, the rise of citizen activism, and the Fourth Industrial Revolution have created a "perfect storm" that is changing our world in ways that we are yet to understand. We are torn between deadly threats, socio-cultural disruptions, and hope that we will prevail. And in the midst of it all, a new phrase has

Design in the Age of Change

emerged in the global vocabulary that captures the spirit of the times—the "new normal."

The "new normal" is a phrase that we now use to describe the new reality in which we all found ourselves. The phrase itself means that in many ways, we have come to grip with things and accepted the fact that our world has changed so dramatically that it will never be the same again. The way we live, work, study, interact with other people, travel, and shop has altered our lives so radically in such an incredibly short period of time, yet the consequences of this massive change will continue to trickle down for years to come.

The issues that we are facing today are far too important for us to simply wait for them to unfold on their own. We need to act—fast. We need to be bold, seek answers, and provide solutions for a better future. But first, we need to imagine a world in which we would actually like to live and work. And this is exactly what designers do best. No other discipline is better equipped when it comes to envisioning future scenarios and in creating a roadmap for achieving them.

I often describe design as a human-centric discipline that acts as the "mirror of society." In many ways, design is a reflection of our understanding of the world in which we live. This reflection is not really an image of how things are, but how we would like them to be. It is fair to say that design today plays a corrective function. Designers often highlight our mistakes and faults and propose new solutions that aspire to make our lives better in some ways—large or small.

Welcome to "The New Normal"

This book represents a snapshot in time—a historical record of how the field of design is experiencing the world right now. Some of the designers featured in this book are global leaders in this field, while others are new and emerging, yet important voices. In their conversations with me, each one of them brings a unique and interesting perspective on our world today, the challenges that we need to overcome, and the ideals that we aspire to achieve.

By looking in the past, and reflecting on the present, these designers project very personal images of the future that they would like to see. The conversations are very broad, and they cover highly diverse topics. From the effects of the pandemic, to issues of race and gender, notions of beauty, technology, and industry, to global and local economies, politics, power, privilege, and the importance of community, in this book we cover all of this, and more.

What is the state of design today?
In conversation with Carole Bilson

The shift to remote working due to the COVID-19 pandemic caught everyone by surprise. At the drop of the hat, most people had to reinvent the way that they were conducting their everyday business. This has caused a great deal of anxiety for everyone, including designers. Once a field firmly established in the way of doing face-to-face business and by having a hands-on approach to work, design had to become a virtual profession overnight. The pandemic has changed the way designers work and has changed the way design is being taught—at least for the time being. But this is not the only shift that we are experiencing in the field of design today. After a long period of "exclusivity" in the field of design, we are now witnessing a push for more diversity and inclusion in design. Like never before, the field of design has finally started embracing women and underrepresented minorities among its professional ranks. This would have never happened if it were not for design leaders such as Carole Bilson paving the way.

Design in the Age of Change

Carole is the most influential woman in the field of design today. As the President of the Design Management Institute (DMI), she represents a community of 30,000 design leaders from more than 60 countries. Prior to this role, she was the first African American woman to become head of global design and user experience at a major corporation, where her team received 49 patents and twelve international design awards. She was also the worldwide product line manager for the Kodak Picturemaker™—a product that has earned the company over a billion dollars. As the leader of DMI, the world's largest community of design and innovation professionals, Carole is uniquely positioned to address the issues that the profession of design is currently facing.

Gjoko Muratovski: Carole, I would like for us to address some of the new realities that we as designers are facing today. We are all experiencing some major changes right now. How would you describe the state of design today?

Carole Bilson: I believe that the longer the pandemic is with us, the changes that we are experiencing are occurring in phases. Its almost like death and dying. In the beginning, everybody's in denial. Nobody really believes that this is happening. And then as the reality starts to sink in, people's behaviors and attitudes change. One thing I can say that I've noticed is that a lot of our members who perhaps have been silent or quiet for a while are reaching out to us. We're getting tremendous communication from around the globe. People want to share their ideas; people want to tune in to listen to what others have to say as a way of learning.

We have also done some small surveys of design leaders. One of the immediate things that we've noticed is that a lot of the medium and large companies have frozen their budgets. Take travel and training; nobody's traveling anywhere, nobody's spending money, very few people are spending money for training. People are looking for free resources and knowledge in order to learn. Those are the immediate things that we see happening, and, of course, there's a lot more going on. There are many challenges for everyone right now, but I think that the current situation also presents great opportunities.

Gjoko Muratovski: How is DMI changing in response?

Carole Bilson: A lot of things, such as the remote working aspect, are causing anxiety in the design community right now. In the beginning of the pandemic, we even offered some workshops on video collaboration because everybody needed to get used to the technology—how to set the lighting, for example, alongside all other aspects of video conferencing. So, we're changing in many ways, and I expect that there will be more changes moving forward. If you listen to the experts, the pandemic is probably going to be around until next year sometime.

Once the pandemic started, we also had to abandon the in-person conferences, which people valued highly. We always got very high marks for our in-person conferences, but we now have to offer our conferences virtually. We've offered other types of virtual programming in the past but now we definitely have to revisit how we are doing this. We need to make the necessary adjustments that everyone is making right now.

Gjoko Muratovski: Designers generally like to have face-to-face experiences. They like to go to workshops and build things, make models, and be very much hands-on.

Carole Bilson: True. Fortunately, most design firms and designers have the necessary digital technology right now. We're lucky that we have these video collaboration tools. We have no choice but to use them. And some people are better at using them than others. All of this is forcing the designers to think more innovatively about how to observe and gather the information that they used to gather in person. So, clearly, this disruption is creating challenges. It's a lot easier to observe and conduct testing in-person than it is through video tools. So, I would say that the shifting is happening in phases. I think that people have gotten over the initial hump of how should they set up and engage via video collaboration. The question now is, "How do they use this tool and other tools to continue to do the work that they used to do?"

Gjoko Muratovski: What are professional designers saying about this new way of working?

Carole Bilson: Most of the design leaders that I've talked to about the impact of COVID-19 on their business say that they are still working and that their clients still want them to do the work. The only difference is that they may be shifting the type of work that they are doing or are reprioritizing things. A couple of days ago, I also had a chance to talk to a corporate executive from a major brand that is in customer experience. She was telling me that they are accelerating all their technology spending and focus around customer experience. So even though she's not a designer, this was encouraging to hear. This is something that will benefit designers working in these areas.

Gjoko Muratovski: There is no doubt that everyone is experiencing the same challenges right now. I also have to say that despite all of this, I do believe that some new opportunities will soon emerge. It has always been the case, historically speaking, that challenges also come with opportunities. With this in mind, what would you say are the new type of opportunities that are emerging within the profession?

Carole Bilson: Well, that's a good question. I'm not sure that I have the exact answer. But my thoughts around that are whenever we're in a crisis, or in a time of extreme stress, this creates an opportunity for us to think differently, to think out of the box. This is also a time for people to try to gain more knowledge, to do research, and to read. I find that I'm reading a lot more than I used to. I find that people are now focusing their time in a different way.

Prior to the pandemic, people were extremely busy. It was very difficult sometimes to get their attention. I am finding now that it's a lot easier to get people's attention because they don't have as many interruptions. They're still busy, but they don't have as many interruptions as they used to have. So you're generally able to get responses from people. People should really use this time to learn, and to do some deep thinking, and to do some experimenting, and to reach out to people perhaps that they wouldn't normally reach out to.

Gjoko Muratovski: Yeah, I notice the same thing about myself, in terms of less distraction. I, too, am now able to dedicate a more concentrated effort on certain things. I also think that designers should use this time to develop new skills or explore new opportunities for themselves. And this goes for design students as well. Many of them are concerned right now about what this disruption will mean to them in terms of their education and future employment opportunities, as they feel that they are missing out on things by not being on campus in a face-to-face mode. I tried to reassure my students that what they will miss in one area, they will gain in another—and that such is life; they will need to learn to adapt.

That is why I started to encourage them right now to learn new skills or strengthen certain other types of skills that will be much more relevant in a remote working environment versus the traditional way we are all used to doing things. And from what I have seen so far, I think the initial results of these efforts are overwhelmingly positive and quite encouraging in terms of the new skills that the students developed and gained in the first few months of the pandemic.

Also, there seems to be another kind of opportunity for many designers in the midst of it all—at least on the corporate side of things. I recently had a conversation with one very large corporation here in the United States regarding their current challenges and opportunities. What they have seen as a positive in this whole thing was that all of a sudden they could now bring in designers on board from all over the world. Before the pandemic, they were only looking at hiring designers that were living in the area where their office was. I think that they were excited about this, as the remote work aspect created a whole new opportunity for them to attract new talent. Prior to COVID-19, they were taking the state of things for granted. This meant that, as a designer, you have to live in the same city as them if you want to work for them. But, now that is no longer an issue. And their talent pool has significantly increased because of that. So yes, we can find some balances here and there.

Carole Bilson: Yeah, and if I can add to that, that's an excellent point. The thing is, though, when you're meeting people for the first time, the jury's still out on how effective this is if you're doing it virtually through a video. It's better to see somebody face-to-face and have a conversation with them when it comes to getting to know them as a person. It's going to be very interesting to see what happens with this over time. But you're absolutely right. This new situation will perhaps allow design services to become more globalized.

Gjoko Muratovski: Carole, I have been following your career for the last few years, and I have seen that you have been a very active advocate for diversity and equity in the profession. I really appreciate all the work that you have done in that area. Can you please tell me more about your own personal experience dealing with diversity challenges?

Carole Bilson: Sure, I'd be happy to. I studied industrial design and graphic design and the early part of my career was primarily focused on industrial design. And then I stepped out of industrial design. I took a program manager role, which was about commercialization. And so I managed multiple disciplines—engineering, supply chain manufacturing design, etc. While all of this experience gave me tremendous opportunities as a woman, I also experienced tremendous hardships in my career. I would probably need a whole day to describe some of the challenges that I experienced along the way. Regardless of this, I learned so much because I think that people learn from positive experiences and they also learn from negative experiences. Whenever I would be in these difficult situations, I would think that I'm learning what not to do when I become a design manager.

Gjoko Muratovski: How did the Diversity in Design initiative come about at DMI?

Carole Bilson: As a result of my life's experiences and the fact that there are so few women in leadership positions, even today, I always had a passion for supporting diversity. I also volunteered heavily as soon as I graduated from college, and I'm a firm believer in giving back to the community. Part of it is my cultural heritage and my family. We just believe very strongly in giving back to the community, as so many people sacrificed for me to be able to do what I'm doing.

I always felt that whenever I can make positive contributions that will hopefully inspire or bring others along. So about four years ago, Jerry Kathman—the Chairman of the Board of DMI at the time—and I were having a conversation and I found out that he was just as passionate about diversity as I was. Jerry was extremely generous, not only with his support for pursuing this initiative but he also offered us the facilities of LPK for us to hold our first *Diversity in Design* conference there. He was also the CEO of LPK at the time; now he is their Chairman. We knew that there weren't that many executive women and people of color. So we had to broaden the umbrella. This allowed us to keep the conference relatively inexpensive and as a result, we were able to attract more people, regardless of their level and their position in the corporate sector.

You can't push forward these kinds of initiatives without strong support, and Jerry gave us that support. LPK, as well as P&G, were really our beginning sponsors. And so we started this *Diversity in Design* conference that we've had now for three years.

We also created the Diversity in Design Manifesto, which is on our website. This manifesto is a guide and an opportunity to hold a mirror up. It's an opportunity to recognize people and companies that are doing constructive and positive things around diversity. In addition to this, we also decided that the third-quarter issue of our *DMI Review* magazine should be focused on promoting diversity—each year. However, the point about that

9

is not that we are only interested in writing about topics on diversity; the point is really to provide a platform for women and people of color to write articles about any topic of interest to them.

They could write about leadership strategy, methods, tools, and case studies. Anything at all they want to share as a way to highlight what they're doing in the field. And I'm so thrilled. This is our fourth year. We'll be coming out with the next issue shortly. And it's just amazing; how these initiatives have brought people to us that we normally wouldn't even know about. We're hearing more voices and more stories.

The whole intention here is that we want to encourage women and people of color. If they're interested in getting into design management or project management, we want to encourage them to pursue their career goals and want them to know that there's a support network within DMI that can help them with that. We have people from whom they can receive mentorship from, bounce ideas off. And we can encourage them to carry on. Otherwise, it can be very lonely and a very discouraging journey if you don't have a support network and you're trying to get ahead.

Gjoko Muratovski: That's great to hear, Carole. I am aware of some of these challenges from some conversations that I had with our Black students and students from other minorities. One of the main things that they have mentioned to me was the lack of mentors and people that they can identify with. This is the case within the university, within the school here, and within the

10

profession, as well—when they pursue internships or when they are starting their employment.

Of the many issues, the lack of Black role models and mentors was one of the things that emerged quite at the top of our discussions. So it's really encouraging to learn that you have set up such a network. And actually, we'll have to follow up with you on that, on a separate note, so that we can integrate that much better with what we do at the Ullman School of Design—especially since I just appointed a new Black design mentor to provide this role here in the school.

Carole Bilson: Absolutely, and Gjoko, if I can just say one more thing. Last year at our *Diversity in Design* conference, we had over one hundred people to attend. One hundred! The first year we had maybe 50. And it's people of all ethnicities. So while most attendees were women and people of color, there were majority people there as well. We had people from all cultures, so the conference was really a microcosm of America. This was an opportunity for everybody to learn. People that are in the majority population could learn from women, could learn from minorities, and the minorities could learn from them, and could meet potential role models and mentors. So, I believe, what you're hearing from the students is that it's very helpful to see people that look like them in leadership roles.

Gjoko Muratovski: Yes.

Carole Bilson: I know that students can get tremendous learning and guidance from the teachers you have now in the school. And that's absolutely fantastic. Most of my mentors early in my career were White men. And that's because that's all that was out there. I have such tremendous respect and fondness for those men that helped me in the beginning of my career, but it certainly is nice to see women and people of color as role models. And they're out there. But it took me three to four years to find them because they aren't that many. Right now most of them are pioneers and there are some tremendously talented and very giving people out there that we yet need to reach out to. They're very busy, of course, but they really appreciate the students and they want to support them in any way that they can. So I appreciate you bringing that up and I would absolutely love to follow up with you later on that.

Gjoko Muratovski: Thank you so much for that, Carole. We are trying to expand our reach and bring different people on board. More and more we realize that we need to do these things on levels that go even beyond race and beyond gender. We need to really embrace a culture that empowers underrepresented voices and gives them a platform to show what they can do. We need a true culture of inclusion. I've been trying to develop this in the school. You have probably seen or heard about some of the things that we have already done. My executive team, for example, is very diverse and we've been trying to bring new diversity initiatives on board whenever we can. And we should never stop doing this. I can never say that we've done enough. It's a constant work-in-progress, for everything we do. It's really encouraging to see that there is an organization such as the DMI that can provide some of these additional support structures and support systems. We could certainly leverage this.

Carole Bilson: Gjoko, I appreciate what you're saying, and I appreciate what you're doing. The mere fact that you're even raising this allows people the opportunity to engage in a dialogue and share what would help them. Because for so long, nobody has asked people like myself what we think about this, or what would be helpful.

Fortunately, things have started to change now. I had an executive of a major company reach out to me and willingly admit, "I'm not a minority; I don't understand the issues that minorities are facing, but I'm willing to admit what I don't know." And he brought a couple of his employees to have a dialogue with us at the DMI about how could they do things a little differently? How could they be more inclusive? And for me, that's so powerful.

This doesn't have to be rocket science. You start out small, and then it just builds over time. It's just like us starting our diversity initiative. When we started this out, I tried to think of how many women and people of color do I know with the title Design Manager, Design Director, Vice President ... And I literally could write down probably five names, if even. So, I rolled up my sleeves, contacted the people I knew, and asked, "Who do you know out there in the design world that is leading, that is doing great things, that we could pull into this circle?" And amazingly, we've been able to find people all over the world.

Design in the Age of Change

While the issues might be a little different in America versus in other regions of the world, the issues are still there—and you're so right about this. I mean, in the United States, for so long Blacks and Hispanics, people of color, have been left out, have been shut out. That's part of what you're seeing coming to the surface now. But generally speaking, around the world, if you create an environment of inclusion where people feel like they're free to speak up and their opinion and their thoughts matter, it totally changes the whole conversation. So, I applaud you and I wish you continued success. And if there is anything that I can do, I'd be happy to help.

Gjoko Muratovski: Thank you, Carole. Thank you so much for everything that you said. I really appreciate that. By the way, earlier in our conversation you mentioned that you had to overcome a lot of challenges in your career. There are other women, other Black women, out there that may be going through the same challenges. It might be helpful for them to hear more about your own journey and the difficulties that you had to face. Would you be comfortable discussing this further?

Carole Bilson: Okay, I will share a little bit about my career, but I have to be honest with you. I'm an eternally optimistic person. An eternally positive person, and I think most designers are. So, a lot of the negative experiences that I had, I kind of buried them. They don't always come to the surface, but I'll at least share a little bit and just walk you through my career.

I studied industrial design and graphic design at the University of Michigan. And then I left there and graduated and I started working as an Industrial Designer. I immediately started to experience some tremendous challenges in the workplace. I mean, all the "isms"—sexism, racism, you name it. Most of it was subtle, and some of it was explicit. Back then people didn't talk about these things. And so you just had to kinda suck it up and keep moving.

I worked at Kodak for thirteen years as an Industrial Designer. I worked on all kinds of products, over 100 types of products. I worked on everything from medical blood analyzers to swimming pool sensors, and cameras of all types—digital and analog. I mean, at that time Kodak had seventeen different business units. I was very fortunate that I got so much design experience in one company because the company had a huge breadth and depth of products. But would you believe that I was working for seven years on so many project teams and it wasn't until I had been working for seven years, that I was in a project meeting with other women? In other words, for seven years, I never saw any women on any of the project teams I was on. And I vividly remember this day. The Project Leader was a woman engineer, and the Human Factors Engineer was a woman. And when everybody left the room, we just started squealing and screaming. We were just so excited to meet each other. Nobody else could appreciate that but us. There is just something about being able to see other people that look like you. It

15

helps you to see that and feel a certain comfort level and role modeling with them.

From there on, I continued to advance at various levels of design. If somebody told me I couldn't do something, I would work overtime if I had to, just to prove them wrong. I was very persistent. I never gave up. Regardless of the negativity, the obstacles that were thrown my way, the sabotage, and all that kind of stuff, I persisted.

Gjoko Muratovski: Thank you for sharing such a personal story with me, Carole. What would be your advice to any new design graduates interested in embarking on a career in design, right now? I know that many design students are worried about the current job market and they're very anxious about it.

Carole Bilson: When I graduated, our economy was in a terrible recession. So even though it was not a pandemic, I experienced the challenge of graduating when there were no jobs and a long recession. The thing I would say is, "Don't be discouraged because these things happen from time to time."

Granted, this is a pandemic. This recession could last maybe a little longer, but you want to make sure you use the time to the best of your ability. If you have not done this already, you should join a professional society; any professional society. You can join the DMI, the Industrial Designers Society of America (IDSA), the American Institute of Graphic Arts (AIGA), etc. There are all kinds of professional design organizations that you can join. Join an organization that you think best fits what your interests are, and then try to get to know some of the people.

I know that everything is virtual now, but you can still look up the members and see who they are and what they do. You can reach out to people that either work where you would like to work or do things that you would like to do. Or, you can go on LinkedIn and look up their background. Here you can see where they went to school and what kind of jobs they had. And if they're alumni from the same school you went to, nine times out of ten they will respond immediately if you send them a note.

If you go on LinkedIn, that's where the business community is primarily. Read the articles that they read. Reach out to people. Network. Make your voice heard. We all were students at one point in time. Have the courage to reach out to people and try to connect with them. These people can give you ideas or help you. Eventually, companies will start hiring again.

Gjoko Muratovski: Carole, thank you for sharing your thoughts and experiences with me. It's always a pleasure talking with you.

Carole Bilson: Thank you, Gjoko. It's has been a real honor. Thank you so much.

What is the future of design?
In conversation with Karim Rashid

Developing a new vision for the future is not an easy task. A visionary leadership requires a special mindset and an attitude. For most people, it is much easier to get entangled in the present, live in the past, or to accept the *status quo* than challenge it. But what happens when the *status quo* ceases to exist? What happens when we have no choice but to look forward? How can we imagine a new way of life, set new standards, and break down existing conventions? How can we be original? Karim Rashid is a designer that has made his career by envisioning new design futures. His work is all about embracing change as it unfolds and reinterpreting it into new spaces, environments, and products.

Karim is one of the most prolific and most recognizable designers of our time. With over 4000 designs in production, more than 300 awards to his name, and clients that span across 40 countries—Karim is a design icon. *TIME* magazine once called him "The Most Famous Industrial Designer in All the Americas." His works are in the permanent collections of the Museum of Modern Art (MoMA) in New York and in San Francisco Museum of Modern Art (SFMOMA), the Cooper Hewitt Smithsonian Design Museum, and the British Design Museum. Earlier this year, Karim received the highest and most prestigious design award in the United States—the 2020 American Prize for Design by the Chicago Athenaeum. This highly coveted award is given to outstanding individuals for their lifetime achievements in the field of design.

Gjoko Muratovski: Karim, I clearly remember when you emerged on the global design scene in the mid 1990s. This was a time when so many things were changing on so many levels. You had this uncanny ability to capture the spirit of the time with your designs. You were very attuned to the zeitgeist that signaled the transition to the new millennium. In your work, you factored in new materials, new software, new technologies, and new social experiences. And you were this very exciting new design voice that was determined to change the world. Now, as we are going through even more radical changes, I'd like to hear how you see the field of design evolving. What does the future of design look like for you?

Karim Rashid: Design for me is always about living in the present. I don't know really where this came from, but I realized that for me to do something original meant that I had to understand the social psychology of the time. I also had to understand the materials of the time, the technologies of the time, and as you mentioned earlier, the software of the time. I had this desire to pull in all those factions and all that criteria in order to do something original. And that's why, let's say back in the 1990s, when you mentioned the things that I was doing, all I was interested in was the moment in which humanity exists.

I was living in the now. I continued that way, and I even continue that way today. I'm not a very nostalgic person. I don't really believe very much in looking back and I don't believe in looking into history. And the reason I don't believe in looking into history is because when we look into history, we're not really designing anymore; even though we say there's something to learn from it. Yes, there's no question there's something to learn from history. But there's a difference between learning and looking at history as a so-called inspiration. The term "inspiration" is a dangerous one because what we do is visual. I'm not really sure you're being inspired when you look at history. If you look back at imagery from the 1960s, and then you make something similar, it's more appropriation or derivation than inspiration.

To be inspired, it's really to be inspired by reading a good book, or hearing good music, or watching the way the person across the street in their window lives day-to-day and how they maneuver around their apartment. That's being inspired. Being inspired is understanding how the mind works, how the human mind operates. Why do we have likes, dislikes? Why do we behave in certain ways? So anyway, to briefly answer your point is that I was obsessed with this notion of doing something original, and in order to do something original, I had to have my tentacles out.

21

Design in the Age of Change

Even now, I have to really feel the moment in which I live, and I have to embrace it. And lastly, I have to be incredibly objective and open-minded. I can't have personal taste, likes, dislikes, and all these things. I have to just be as if I come from another planet. I've been telling myself, for 25–30 years now, that I should always just act as if I come from a different place, another planet, and watch humanity. Because humanity is funny, strange, it's peculiar and it's maudlin, it's ... I don't know how to say this ... it's kitsch sometimes. It's loaded. You have to step back and look at the issue, look at the problem, look at what you're working on. And there's so much opportunity to be inspired by. And in turn, when you bring those things in, you will do something original.

Now is 2020, and as you said, we are going through a very major change. There's going to be a massive schism here. First schism was the introduction of the digital age because the digital age is a dematerialization. It's not about doing physical stuff. It's not about designing physical things such as clothes, objects, architecture ... anything, really. Digital age is immaterial, right? So that was the first big, big shift. And the second big shift is that digital age has shown us how we can now globally operate with almost no physicality whatsoever. The virus has directly impacted and exponentially grown, this virtual human realm. My physicality with you right now is basically my laptop, that's it. My other physicality is— because I needed a good cup of coffee—my coffee mug in my hand, or my eyeglasses on my head, or my elbows that are on the table. All our human experiences, let's

22

say, our evolution, our progress or innovation, it's all happening digitally at this moment in time.

Gjoko Muratovski: Well, you're essentially describing our gateway into Industry 4.0. All of this, without a doubt, will cause major and permanent changes to our lives. In fact, by 2030, it is believed that the rise of technological advances brought to us by the Fourth Industrial Revolution will displace many of the existing job functions and will replace them with completely new ones. And this is already happening. The pandemic has just fast-tracked this whole thing. COVID-19 has skyrocketed us into this digital world sooner than we were prepared. And this, I think, is an interesting conversation.

This will impact the type of skills that people need to have in a world that is dominated by technology. And I think that this is fascinating to observe, because the more technology starts dominating the world, the more the need for people who can understand what it means to be human will come to the forefront. And designers, as being human-centric in their core, are really well positioned to help define this new world. Because, when anything technological is possible, it's no longer a question of "Can we do this?" It's a question of "Why do we need to do this?"

Karim Rashid: Yeah!

Gjoko Muratovski: The reason why I thought that you would be such a great person to be talking on the topic of "new normal" is precisely because of what you explained in the beginning, about how you were looking at the world when you started your career, and how you continue looking at the world today. After all, the notion of "new normal" just implies that we are coming to grips with the reality of things. This means that we now accept that the world is no longer going to be the same. But it's not an easy thing to do this. It's very hard to just detach yourself and embrace this whole new change. And this is why I really wanted to understand what this "new normal" means to you right now, because you have this ability to see the world in this way.

Karim Rashid: Well, of course, it's difficult because we are human beings; we are social animals. At the end of the day, you could argue that the only reason we exist on this planet is for each other. If we don't have each other what do we have? And that goes back to issues of relationships, love, and family—all these things. So obviously, the difficult part right now is a lack of—let's be honest—the lack of physical contact. Right? That's really what's going on in a way.

Gjoko Muratovski: That's a wonderful take on things, Karim. Design should always be in the service of humanity. We do need to question designs that stand in the way of what makes us human. Let us expand our conversation a little bit. Tell me more about your pursuit of originality.

Karim Rashid: A pursuit of originality is something that I grappled with for many, many years in my life. When

What is the future of design?

I was a little child, I was a bit of a non-conformist and I was ridiculed constantly and all that. I always felt like the odd child. And as a result, I always had this need to somehow gain some sort of respect. I was the best drawer in the class. I was one of the top students in mathematics. I was pushing, as a child, to prove to my peers that I have some value, or meaning, or something. But you know, at that time, I noticed that education was, and still is, this idea of introducing the lowest common denominator as a base level—a platform intended to make us all be the same from a very young age. And when you're pushed to be the same in your formative years, this stuff sticks with you for the rest of your life.

One day, when my child—my daughter—was in pre-K, I went to pick her up and a little boy walked up to me (he was about 4 years old) and said, "Why do you paint your nails?" And my instant reaction to that little child was, "Why not?" But when I walked away, I thought to myself that he'd go back home and tell his family, father or mother, about me. Then, probably his father would say, "That's ridiculous—why would a man paint his nails?" And there's this ongoing—even in 2020— an ongoing, perverse, desirous need to be like everybody else, to fit in.

It's like as if human beings are phenomenally inse-cure. But when you think about it, historically, it was the creative people that were always exiled. Right? They were often executed. They were thrown out of their com-munities. This notion of being creative and being differ-ent was almost non-permitted throughout history. But those people that were trying to break out of the norm

25

were always put under a phenomenal amount of pressure to suppress their real existence. And if you are one of those people, and you have that creative part inside you, then your soul is telling you, "I am on this earth with a different fingerprint than everybody else."

Gjoko Muratovski: People who chose to become designers, or architects, or artists, often do so because they very strongly feel the need to create, to leave their mark on the world in some way.

Karim Rashid: Yes! I am here to create something, and I have said this for many years, "To be is to create." We are all given the genes to create. Look at the progress of humanity. Look at the material world around us. This is all creation. We've created all this. To put this in other words, the whole world is designed. Period.

As designers, we shape the future of humanity. If I, tomorrow, design a building, that building may be around for 50 years. So I am shaping human experiences for the next 50 years. This is also why I have to be sensitive and cautious with my work, and how can I say ... responsible. We have to be sensitive to the moment in which we live. And we are living in a very strange new world right now.

Gjoko Muratovski: What would you describe as inspirational designs?

Karim Rashid: There are so many things to be inspired by if you look at the history of design. Say, Charles and

What is the future of design?

Ray Eames. They designed the famous "potato chip" chair. Why is this chair iconic? It's not because it was produced in Michigan by Herman Miller. It's because it was the first time that plywood was bent in 3D. That's what made it pivotal in the world of design. It made a big shift and that's why it's an icon.

Alvar Aalto designed another iconic chair before this. He designed the first chair that was done in 2D bentwood, for example. Mart Stam and Marcel Breuer designed the first-ever tubular chair. They saw a bicycle factory in Dresden that was bending steel tubes, and they said, "Hey, maybe we can make a chair like this." After seventeen prototypes later they managed to get a chair that we now know as so famous. The Louis Ghost chair of Kartell by Philippe Starck is the first time a poly-carbonate molded injection chair was made. Hence, it became iconic. All of these objects have made an impact and there are thousands of inspirations out there just like these.

Gjoko Muratovski: I think that moving forward, Gener-ative Design technology is going to change things rad-ically. At the Ullman School of Design we have a very close relationship with Autodesk, who are the the leaders in Generative Design technology. We were actually very fortunate to have access to this technology, probably a year before anyone in the industry had access to is. You know, sometimes Autodesk allow us to play around with things like this so that we can explore the untapped potential of new technologies. So I had this idea of using this technology to create the first Generative Design chair. At the time, I had a conversation with Magis about this. I think at one point you did a project with them as well.

So, I visited their headquarters in Venice. We also met in New York, as well. And so I said, "Hey guys, let's create together the first Generative Design chair. Let's use the Autodesk software to do this and see what the artificial intelligence will come up with." Now, the artificial intelligence doesn't actually design the chair. But it generates hundreds of thousands of possible solutions. And it's very interesting how the role of the designer actually changes during the process of co-creating designs together with a machine. The designer moves away from the typical exploratory process, which calls for endless sketching and modeling until a certain shape is formed. The computer does that part now. The role of the designer moves away from that part and the designer transitions from being a creator to becoming a curator. So as a designer you're curating the way the machine is designing, except the machine can generate hundreds of thousands of solutions in a matter of seconds, which is humanly impossible. What you do as a designer is, you set parameters that create a framework for this process. For example, you can tell the computer to use certain materials, manufacturing processes, you can set specific dimensions for the object, and you can even set the manufacturing cost. Then you get a computer-generated concept based on your input, which can then be 3D printed on demand. I thought that this is a pretty great idea, especially since this can change completely how furniture is designed and made. And there is also no need to store these chairs in a warehouse if you can produce them on demand. However, it was difficult for Magis to grasp this because they really believe in the idea that they need people to design and craft things. So they didn't go for it. Then, a year later, Philippe Starck developed the first Generative Design chair with Kartell—also in partnership with Autodesk.

I was so disappointed that Magis passed on this opportunity.

Karim Rashid: Yeah, well, it doesn't always matter if you're the first or not. What I mean is that originality and being first are not necessarily completely symbiotic.

Gjoko Muratovski: I understand that ... For me it was more about being present in the moment. We had access to this technology right then. It was new and Magis had not seen anything like it. I understand that this was radically different to anything that they have done before, but they should have just embraced the opportunity to experiment and create something radically new.

Karim Rashid: You should continue experimenting with this technology. I always say that as designers we are editors of social change, and we're cultural shapers. And we're the ones who move this world. And we create the movements that become the trends. They become the kind of social milieu of the time, always, you know.

With all that said, let's talk about something ...

Here we are living in this virtual age. Maybe this is an opportunity to finally make the world more disparate or to create more choices. The world is shrinking and our

29

culture is increasingly becoming singular. And that singular culture is constantly appropriated across the globe. Nowadays, except for the last six months due to the pandemic, I was flying 200 days a year. I was in cities around the world and what do I see? I hear the same music, I see the same furniture, I see the same interiors, and I see the same skyscrapers. I see the same people drinking the same cocktails. I see the sameness. Basically, what I'm seeing is a world shrinking to the point of perpetual "me too-ism." Perpetual. That's it. But what happened? Is there an avant-garde anymore?

The perversity is that we have all these amazing tools and software that are basically democratic. I mean, this stuff is so free for everybody. We can do anything. There are tens of thousands of musicians—more musicians today than ever before in history. There are more designers and artists than ever before in history. This is the creative epoch. Everybody decides now they're going to be creative, right? And this we are all capable of, which is fantastic. So on the one hand, humanities have gone in the right direction. We are all capable of creativity. At one time, creativity was suppressed. Now we're becoming freer, and freer, and freer to be self-expressive, to find ourselves, to be different, to be creative, and the paradox is—that's not happening.

Gjoko Muratovski: Yeah, there was the same criticism about architecture, as well. We are experiencing McDonaldization of cities. For more than 20 years now, star architects are just replicating their own buildings, city across city, around the world. The paradox is that

What is the future of design?

cities are commissioning star architects because they are trying to be unique, but they all end up looking the same.

Karim Rashid: Right. Yes! It's true. It's like all the thinkers for the city and the mayor, go: "How are we going to attract tourism? Let's see, what should we do? Well, let's hire this architect, you know. Yeah, Paris did this. We'll do it. You know, Bilbao in Spain did it, we'll do it too." You know, I find this to be ridiculous. This perpetual following frustrates me. But I will say this, and I think that deep down this is my greatest inspiration: The things that frustrate me, the things that I dislike, the things that don't work around me, makes me want to do better. Makes me want to fix them. Makes me want to do something different.

Gjoko Muratovski: I think that every designer inherently has these feelings. And this is a common thread that I have noticed. You take any designer, you unpack them, and you will find that drive within them. I always find this very interesting—the designers' need to constantly change the world and improve it. This "I can do better" attitude that designers have is essentially about making the world a better place—from the smallest to the biggest thing.

Karim Rashid: The key is that designers have to believe in that social agenda, but I don't think that all designers are actually that socially inclined. I think a lot of times in their mind some designers are playing games or tricks or doing something that they think is expressive. One design movement that opened the doors for doing a lot of bad work out there—and I hate to criticize it, but I'll be the only person in the world to criticize it—it's the Dutch design movement, Droog. They basically have this notion that design is about one-liners. So that you go and you say, "Oh! That's nice. Campari bottles making a lamp! Rope that becomes a chair? Oh, That's nice." You know, you could argue that this kind of design is bordered on kitsch.

Gjoko Muratovski: Well, these kinds of works are not really design. They are gimmicks.

Karim Rashid: Yeah. And I am shocked by the majority of it. It's very superficial. It's not very smart, not pushing anything, not deep, not thinking even about how this stuff is physically built. And there's too much stuff in the world anyway, right? So as a designer, as we said earlier, you are also an editor. And I would say that a good designer should get rid of three things by putting one new thing on the market. A kind of, addition by subtraction, let's call it. So if I add to the world, I also try to subtract a little bit from the world.

Gjoko Muratovski: I like that. That's a really good way to look at things.

Karim Rashid: Yeah, the world can't take on more things anymore. We can't keep producing and producing endlessly. To me, this is the other social shift that's happening in the world right now. Look at retail. Retail has been dying for years. In fact, many industries were dying even before the virus. And as you mentioned, the virus now is almost like the eye of the storm. And boom! Now retail is really dead, all of a sudden. You walk on Madison Avenue here in New York and Fifth Avenue and every other shop is now abandoned.

After this pandemic ends, I hope that we're going to consume less, but better. That's an old saying—maybe Dieter Rams said that—but less is better. And we're going to move to that because we are now learning something new. We're learning that we can live with less. Dematerialization is very good for humanity. And you know what? It's the only way we're going to survive. We got to slow down. We all got to pull back. We got to be more resourceful. We got to be smarter. We have to let the earth survive.

This doesn't mean that we should regress and go back to living off the land and not having technology. No, we need to use our new technologies and start creating a world that's sustainable, that's smart, that can afford us to have great human experiences with a lot less.

Gjoko Muratovski: It's very interesting that you mentioned this. Actually, at the moment, I'm working within the AgTech sector with one smart farming company that uses artificial intelligence and predictive analytics to grow crops, and I can say that this is the future. This is an incredible new territory for designers and for technology companies to explore. There are so many challenges within the existing agricultural practices. The world keeps growing and growing and more and more people need to be fed. Yet, we need to produce a huge amount of food with very little of the resources that we are currently using.

Karim Rashid: Right. Most important thing is just moving forward—for everyone. In fact, we need smart fashion as well. Clothing eventually should be made on demand. Once we have that in place the reduction in consumption of energy will be phenomenal.

Gjoko Muratovski: A couple of years ago, I was having a conversation with Amazon about re-imagining the future of retail and introducing fashion on demand. So the way that we are seeing this is that retail may not be a place where you go to buy the clothes. The physical space itself, I mean. But maybe, the retail place will have a large 3D scanner, where you go to create a digital imprint of yourself, and then also view samples of various fabrics and materials. So your scan becomes your brand avatar and then you choose the type of fabrics that you like, colors, and so on, and then whenever you want to order something, a piece of clothing is delivered to you, that is just for you. This is much better than having these random things sent to you instead, that you then have to ship back because they don't fit you just right.

Karim Rashid: There are lots of startups working on this. In the last five years, I was approached by three different startups to do this. No one's put it out there yet.

You know, in 1999, I was doing a flagship shop for Giorgio Armani. First interior I got. I was very

What is the future of design?

impressed he even gave me one because I was an industrial designer. I flew to Milan, he met with me, and he said, "You know, I want to reinvent myself for the twenty-first century." He said, "You're the guy to do it for me." I was very much like, "Yeah!" I mean, it's great, right? [Laughs] So, I proposed to him to launch one shop in New York, one in Tokyo, and one in Paris. Each one was based on a different idea. The one in New York, for example, had a runway. And basically, models would walk around all day in the store modeling on the runway. Also, when you walk in, you'll see a huge flat screen and a body scanner. This is in 1999, by the way. The reason why I have proposed this is because just before that I was at SIGGRAPH in New Orleans and I saw the body scanners there. They showed them and at that time they were maybe $250,000 each. Crazy money. But this was the beginning of the idea. I wanted to put a body scanner in which you could walk in and then use touch screens to try on 30 years of Giorgio Armani fashion archives.

At SIGGRAPH, they scanned me and replaced John Travolta with me in the movie *Saturday Night Fever*. It was hilarious. And I was so impressed with that. Right? That was 1999. It hasn't happened yet. But I do think we'll use this technology in retail stores as well at some point.

Gjoko Muratovski: People are working on this. Currently, the fashion industry is very focused on this kind of personalized fashion. This will happen because companies are losing a lot of money by not doing this. There is too much waste and too much unnecessary production. And

35

often when you order something online, you try it on, and
you return it because it doesn't fit you. This is costing the
industry a lot of money. So that is why I think that this will
happen.

Karim Rashid: Yeah! Can I also add something to what you
were saying about all of these non-serial, on-demand pro-
ductions? We also touched on this in the beginning of our
conversation, with the artificial intelligence designed chair.

Gjoko Muratovski: Of course.

Karim Rashid: So, back in the day, I was very impressed
with Gaetano Pesce. Do you know who he is?

Gjoko Muratovski: Oh, yes.

Karim Rashid: Okay, so you know. Yes. He was my professor back in the early 1980s when I was studying in
Italy.

Gaetano did a lot of experiments over the years, and, in
New York, he was basically trying to create a non-serialized
production line. He had workers make a mold, and he'd
have all these cans of paint holding different colors being
raised above the mold, and the workers would pull strings
and fill the mold with the color of their choice. Because the
paint would randomly fill the mold, every chair, every table
that came out was completely different—but at the same
time, it was still an assembly line of sorts.

Then he made a wooden box with a shape of a chair
inside and he will inject polyurethane in the box to make

chairs. But the polyurethane didn't quite reach all the surfaces. So every chair that came out looked like it was from the Stone Age and had completely different shapes. I was so inspired by this notion of non-serialization. But when I finally got a chance to try to do some things like this, Computer Numerical Control (CNC) machines were already available. They were about a million dollars apiece, but they were available.

I experimented with a machine like this down in Santa Fe, New Mexico, when I worked for a company called Nambe. You take a piece of alloy, put it on the machine, and then you cut any shape you want. Nambe loved this idea. They opened up a little factory and we were making a lot of designs—salt and pepper shakers, creamers, vases, and all kinds of things—over a period of three to four years. So one day I thought, "What if we find someone who could write a software program so that the machine will randomly cut its own boss?" So we did that. The machine cut 30 vases one day, in a period of about two hours. We put them all in a row and looked at them all and they all had completely different forms. The machine cut weird vases. And I loved this, because it was like, it's like what you talked about in the beginning. I am now the curator and the editor. We put the vases in boxes and there are bunches of boxes on the shelves now, but the vase you see on the box is not the vase you'll get inside the box.

Gjoko Muratovski: Yeah, actually, I remember that. Now that you mentioned it, I remember this project that you did. It didn't work out, right? I think the frustration with the people was that they were buying something that is not what they've actually seen on the box.

Karim Rashid: Yeah ... The customers got so disappointed. We were selling these at Bloomingdale's, right? So I went to Bloomingdale's. And I sat there signing some objects and all that, and a woman saw the box with the vase there. She opened the box and was confused. I tried to explain the process and then I realized that the problem was that we had to educate the people about the idea first. And it was such a disaster. It was such a mark-a-bomb, you know.

Gjoko Muratovski: I find this very interesting. Actually, if you look at this from another perspective, then you will see that this actually was a really great project. People today are much more receptive to personalization in design. In any case, at the end of the day, it's all about setting the right expectations.

Karim Rashid: Yes. Today you could do this.

Gjoko Muratovski: You absolutely could. I think that if you come with the right mindset to the store, then it's almost like unpacking a present. You don't know what you're getting, but it's exciting. The surprise factor adds to customer experience. And this is unique. Nobody else is will have the exact same object as well, which adds further to its value.

Karim Rashid: Yeah, exactly! And you know what's interesting about it? Even though the vases were unique, they cost the price of sameness. Getting this vase was $60. The vases were all priced the same. So that was the interesting thing here. There was a time when for uniqueness you always had to pay luxury or premium. This project was challenging all those myths of the idea that you should pay more for something that's unique. Today you can produce uniqueness that is democratic.

Gjoko Muratovski: This whole thing reminds me of one creativity exercise. A friend of mine was once doing this workshop on creativity with restaurant owners. And it's a very fascinating exercise, because it shows how people have this set framework for everything, and it also shows how difficult it is for people to step away from this.

So, he ask a group of restaurant owners, "Tell me at least ten things that any restaurant must have, no matter what." And then they say something like, tables, chairs, kitchen, menu, cutlery, you know—whatever. They list various things. And he says, "Okay. Now take away one of these items and tell me how you're going to run a restaurant without it." And they say, "Impossible, you absolutely need all of these things in a restaurant." He presses on and says, "Let's take away the menu, for example. Let's say that your restaurant will have no menu. How would you run your restaurant?" And their answer is that this is impossible. "How will people know what to order?" He then asked, "Why do you think this is an issue? When people come to your home as guests for

39

dinner, do you give them a menu? No. Were they upset with the food that you brought them? No. Were they enjoying their experience visiting you? Yes. Well, there you go."

It's possible to create a great experience with any scenario as long as you set the right expectations from the start. And what ordinary people see as a limitation, creative people see as an opportunity.

Karim Rashid: There's a quotient or interesting change like this that took place during the pandemic. I went to a couple of cafes here in New York just recently because they're all open if you sit outdoors. And they basically have a QR code on the table and you can trace the QR code to access the menu with your phone. Now, I have made that proposal in the last ten years to about twenty restaurants that I've designed. And nobody—no restaurant owner—was the least bit interested in making a menu virtual on your phone. And that now is going to be a given. And another thing that is interesting, in line with this, is that more and more we are touching less.

Gjoko Muratovski: There are so many new things that are going to come out of this pandemic. There will be many new opportunities for designers to explore next. I guess this is at least some kind of silver lining that we have in this whole unfortunate scenario.

What is the future of design?

Karim Rashid: Yeah. And I hope that next time you and I will have a conversation like this it will be in person.

Gjoko Muratovski: I hope so.

Why do we need creativity now more than ever?
In conversation with Natalie Nixon

When we are faced with new and unforeseen challenges, such as the ones that we're experiencing today, we don't really have ready-made solutions at hand to help us overcome these challenges. We need to envision new solutions and generate new and original ideas. In other words, we need to be creative. This is important because creativity is the source of all innovation. But how can we cultivate it? Natalie Nixon studies the role that creativity plays in our lives and the ways in which organizations can embrace their creative side.

Natalie is a design thinker, creativity strategist, and a Fellow of the London-based Royal Society of Arts. She is also a contributor to *Inc. Magazine* and a member of the Forbes Councils. Natalie incorporates her background in anthropology, foresight, fashion, and design management, and uses her cross-cultural experiences of living and working around the world to inform her

43

approach to creativity. She is also the award-winning author of *The Creativity Leap*—one of the Top 40 business books of 2020.

Gjoko Muratovski: Some people describe creativity as a way of living life that embraces originality and makes unique connections between seemingly disparate ideas. Others describe creativity as an ability to invent or create something new. This is a particularly important skill to have, especially in terms of global disruption. So let's start with the basics, Natalie. How can we best define creativity?

Natalie Nixon: I love both of those definitions, Gjoko, because they talk about inventiveness and originality, and how we approach problems. I personally like to think that creativity is our ability to toggle between wonder and rigor to solve problems. A key output of creativity is the production of novel value. In this regard, creativity acts as the engine for innovation.

Gjoko Muratovski: Why is creativity such an essential competency, especially today?

Natalie Nixon: Creativity is an essential competency today because we are living in a world that's volatile, uncertain, complex, and ambiguous. And specifically in this moment, Gjoko—you and I are talking in early November of the year 2020—we are going through what I call a triple pandemic. It's not just the virus pandemic that is affecting us in terms of our health; we also have a

44

pandemic of societal and environmental issues that we are facing, as well. And the truth is, we're not going to be able to navigate such complexity with a simple linear Gantt chart. You will quickly become very frustrated if you try to apply that sort of linear process to addressing complex questions. The best way to navigate complexity is with complexity, and creativity is a complex system.

Gjoko Muratovski: Creativity, as you describe it, is the very essence that drives innovation. How would you explain the relationship between creativity and innovation?

Natalie Nixon: Yeah, that's a great question. When I say that creativity is the engine for innovation, I guess I should first pause and give my opinion on what innovation is. I think that innovation is invention converted into value. That value could be financial, social, or cultural. Invention on its own is not an innovation. Invention needs a conversion process and that converter is creativity.

I'll give an example. I went to the Post Office the other day. When I got to the counter, there was the usual Plexiglas barrier set up, due to COVID-19. Then, I noticed in front of me a container of Q-tips ear swabs. I thought to myself, why are there ear swabs at the Post Office counter? And then I asked the gentleman at the counter, "Excuse me, why are there Q-tips in the front?" He said, "Oh, that's because of the pandemic and is for people to pick up one and they can tap the credit card keypad with the Q-tip instead of with their finger."

Now, that's a clever invention, right? This person saw a need and identified a solution. People want to avoid touching things because they don't want to get their skin contaminated. So he provided the customers with a little swab that they could use instead. That's a clever invention, but that's not an innovation. And it won't become an innovation until it actually creates value at scale.

Two months later, I'm flipping through a catalog and I see a key ring for sale that also has a hook and a pointer that people can use during the time of COVID-19 to open doors or push keypads. So here's someone who saw a similar problem. But now they have developed a product that is being manufactured at scale. In this case, this innovation has the potential to produce some sort of financial value for the company that has come up with this invention, while producing value for the customers, as well.

So that's how I see the relationship between creativity and innovation. Perhaps I should say invention, creativity, and innovation. They're all interrelated, but they are distinct.

Gjoko Muratovski: This is a pretty good example, actually. And I think that we will see more and more of these types of inventions/innovations coming up. I think that people are particularly good at coming up with new, innovative ways of dealing with problems in a state of crisis. Innovation often comes from a sheer necessity that forces you to just revisit your everyday life.

Natalie Nixon: Yes. Absolutely. I like to say that creativity loves constraints. It loves constraints on time, constraints on money, and constraints on people's resources. It's almost like we need that "pressure cooker effect" in order to drive inventiveness, and to be more resourceful, and to juxtapose things, objects, and ideas that previously we would have never put together.

Gjoko Muratovski: I find that the same thing applies to design in general. As a designer, the worst thing I can think of is to be faced with a blank canvas followed with the request, "Come up with something." Designers need problems to solve and obstacles to overcome. And the core skill that designers use to do this is creativity.

What I find interesting now is that many reports on Industry 4.0 say that the demand for creativity, as a key "soft" skill, is expected to grow significantly across all job sectors in the near future. As automation and artificial intelligence replace more and more jobs, the ability to think creatively will be considered as one of the most critical skills for future industry leaders. What are your thoughts on this?

Natalie Nixon: I have a lot of thoughts on this. About five years ago, in 2015, when the World Economic Forum started producing such reports, they said that creativity would become the "Number Ten" job skill by 2021, in terms of importance to industry. A year later, in 2016, they corrected themselves and said that actually they expect creativity to become the "Number Three" job skill by 2021.

And the truth of the matter is that the train has left the station—we are already in the Fourth Industrial

Revolution. And what the Fourth Industrial Revolution is characterized by the notion that technology is everywhere; it's ubiquitous. It's not all a rosy picture, but it's not all frightening either. Artificial intelligence and augmented reality are already here—people order things through Alexa, and surgeries are done through robotics. All of these things come with some casualties. Some jobs will be lost. And in my view, the opportunity is that as technology is replacing a lot of tasks, there will be more opportunities for the "human" to show up in our organizations and in our work. Now is the time for us to start figuring out how to hire for creativity, how to cultivate creativity, and how to sustain it.

Fifteen years ago, people used to say that if you are not a tech company—whether you are in education, healthcare, food and beverage, or whatever—then you will not last long. Every organization had to figure out how to integrate technology into their core value proposition. Today, in my opinion, if you're not a creativity company, you're in trouble. Whatever your industry is, it doesn't matter; creativity has to be the core of what you do.

And I realize that there's artificial imagination. I realize that there's intuitive machinery. I get all that. However, there are certain irreplaceable aspects and dimensions of being human that we have to amplify moving forward. Creativity is one of those aspects.

Gjoko Muratovski: I absolutely agree with you. Let's expand on things a bit more. What would you say are some of the key factors that drive creativity?

48

Why do we need creativity now more than ever?

Natalie Nixon: When I was writing my book, *The Creativity Leap*, I interviewed over 50 people who came from diverse industry sectors to understand how they apply creativity in their work. And I realized that improvisation, intuition, and inquiry—or curiosity—are the three key elements that drive creativity.

Also, things that help in this process include asking new questions—different questions, and better questions. I'm a big fan of the work of Warren Berger who wrote the book *A More Beautiful Question,* where he talks about how asking questions is a way of thinking. We can exercise creativity as a skill by not being afraid to ask new and different questions. This also means that in our educational environments, we have to shift away from being solution oriented, in terms of pursuing that one correct answer. What we really need to do is to encourage questions and curiosity instead.

Another element that helps to drive creativity is working with people who are different from you. Building teams that have cognitive diversity is particularly important. Working in a diverse environment will require you to learn more, and this will allow you to unpack and redefine the way you think about things.

Gjoko Muratovski: What is the biggest misconception that you have come across when it comes to what people think about creativity?

Natalie Nixon: I find that the biggest misconception is the assumption that there are people who are "creative types." It's this misconception that there is this hallowed,

49

special group of people who are imbued with creativity. And when you really start to dig deeper into this, then you realize that when people say that, they are actually talking about artists. And this is a problem. Our society has ghettoized creativity and the arts.

Yes, artists are using creativity to the maximum level, but creativity and arts are not the same thing. Creativity is the means to that end. Creativity is the means to becoming an incredible artist; but it is also the means to becoming an incredible engineer, entrepreneur, farmer, teacher, plumber ... anything, really. But most people don't think of creativity in these terms. Instead, most people think that artists have the sole ownership of creativity. And this is the biggest misconception that I have come across.

When we make this assumption, we are letting ourselves off the hook. And it's not fair to the artists, either. What artists are exceptional at, and what they're excellent at, is the way they wrestle with the discomfort and the ambiguity of the process. Creativity is hard work, and that's what a lot of us don't really want to accept. Most people don't really want to engage with creativity as a process, because this can be hard and frustrating at times. Great solutions and great ideas don't come easy. Not everything comes with a clear "yes" or "no" answer.

You have to sit with the idea and then you have to walk away and zoom out, and then you have to bring people in who have different perspectives than you. And when that fails, you have to go into your own zone again and try something else. Designers go through this process in studio critiques, and so do the visual artists. The performing arts do this through their recitals. We do this in manufacturing by showing our works in progress and reflecting on them. This is a very difficult thing to do. But these tough moments have to exist. They are part of this process. They can be unpleasant, scary, and terrifying, but at the end, you have to show your creation to the world. People may reject it, but may be they will love it. The fear of what that answer is going to be is what is holding people back from embracing their creativity.

So the biggest misconception is that when people say that they are not creative because of whatever reason, is really not acceptable to me. We are all born to be hardwired for creativity. The difference is whether or not you are finding the time to exercise your creativity, or you're being lazy about it, and you're not putting in the time. Artists are creative because they put in the time. And that's the only difference.

Gjoko Muratovski: You're absolutely correct, Natalie. Most people think that creativity is a natural-born talent—you either have it, or you don't. But the reality is that creativity can be taught and can be practiced. And yes, it requires a lot of work to master a new skill to perform it in its excellence. And creativity is just that; a skill like any other.

I often wonder where this misconception comes from, and I think that for most people, this is something that is rooted in childhood. I think that most children lose their creative spark during their formative years. In many cases, children are often discouraged by their parents, friends, and even their schoolteachers, from exercising their creativity. Instead, their attempts to be creative are criticized, or made fun of. Instead, children are asked to fall in line and be like everyone else. I think that in our

51

society, teaching children how to be like everyone else is more important than allowing them to explore.

Natalie Nixon: I've had grown people share painful memories about a teacher who told them that they are no good at something. That's awful. Why would you do that to a child? These people are now middle-aged men, and they still haven't forgotten this. And sometimes we get messages like that from our parents, who simply are trying to look out for us by telling us to be more practical instead. But what's practical; anything that is seemingly logical and can make you money?

Gjoko Muratovski: At the beginning of our conversation, you mentioned that creativity sits between wonder and rigor. What did you mean by that?

Natalie Nixon: I often like to say, "Wonder is found in the midst of rigor, but rigor cannot be sustained without wonder." By wonder, I mean things such as awe, dreaming, and asking really big, blue-sky, audacious questions. Wonder is also about allowing yourself to be inspired, which in the United States, we're not really good at. [Laughs] We're not good at all at taking a break, or a pause to think and reflect. And without pausing to think, you can't get perspective. Rigor, on the other hand, is about discipline. This is all about spending time on the task at hand. It's about development, and about paying attention to the details. Rigor is not sexy. It's often very solitary. But this is the only way that you create the structure and the boundaries that you need in order to be productive.

Why do we need creativity now more than ever?

Without wonder, you burn out. By combining both, you will become not only productive, but creative as well.

Gjoko Muratovski: That is really well put. And I agree with you that we need to allow ourselves the time to be creative.

Natalie Nixon: Yes. Pursuing innovation by following prescribed processes is not going to get you there.

Gjoko Muratovski: True. I see this as an issue when it comes to design thinking, because most people practice design thinking by following a prescribed process. This is not how design thinking really works in practice. This only works in theory. In real life, there are no prescribed processes. You just need to embrace things as they unfold in front of you.

Natalie Nixon: Well, the most important thing in design thinking is the process of iteration. And this process is not a straight line. Iterations are very much dependent on context; they are situational. You have to be adaptive and flexible, and it takes practice and experience. And over time, you get better at it.

Gjoko Muratovski: Natalie, thank you so much for your insights. I really enjoyed the conversation with you. Thank you!

Natalie Nixon: Gjoko, thank you for having me as a guest.

How can we change ... everything?
In conversation with Bruce Mau

Psychology studies show that when people are in a state of chaos they can form new habits more easily. When our lives go haywire, the key elements that influence our behaviors in the environment in which we live tend to disappear. This new state of things creates a profound opportunity for reinvention. There has been a lot of research in this area, which is referred to as "habit discontinuity." According to the theory in this field, when people are undergoing some kind of massive change—a life disruption of some kind—they are also exposed to the opportunity to try out new things that they perhaps didn't have a chance to do before and are forced to stop doing things that they used to do. As a result, these moments create the best pre-conditions for people to break old habits and form new ones.

Nevertheless, most people fear that when they are faced with stressful and uncertain situations, nothing good will come out from change, which is why they often avoid making new decisions in their life and work. In reality, during times of uncertainty most people tend to act more authentically on their values and they end up making decisions that are better for them in the long run. This happens because in such situations, people tend to ask themselves more fundamental questions such as, "Do I want to do this? How do I do this? What are my new choices here?" This is an opportunity for people to rethink the decisions that they were making in their lives until that point. When faced with such critical situations, people act in ways that are consistent not with "who they are," but "who they want to be," and this experience can be quite transformative. We, as a society, are now in a situation just like this. And as such, we are in a position to define what this change that we are experiencing today means for us, on an individual level and as a collective.

One person that has explored this topic for many years is Bruce Mau. Bruce, however, is not a psychologist; he is a designer. But he is not what people would call a "typical designer." He designs books and cities, carpets and social programs, global brands, and cultural institutions. He had a stellar career in the field over the last several decades, and his name is firmly embedded in the annals of design. In addition to his many awards and accolades, he is also named as an Honorary Royal Designer for Industry by the Royal Society of Arts. His books *S,M,L,XL* (with Rem Koolhaas), *Life Style*, *Massive Change*, and *MC24: Bruce Mau's 24 Principles for Designing Massive Change in your Life and Work* are widely read and have received both cult status and critical acclaim.

Gjoko Muratovski: Bruce, let's talk about change. Most people fear change. Change is disruptive and change can cause a great deal of anxiety, even when it is on a small scale. But change can also be a good thing. How do you view this period of massive change that we are experiencing right now?

Bruce Mau: If you think about where we are right now in the long sweep of history, then you will realize that we are facing challenges that are of an order of magnitude and complexity that we've never had to deal with before. Over the coming decades, and I think more urgently over the coming years, we will experience a change of an unprecedented scale. We will experience a profound change in the ways that we live and work. As a designer, I am committed to making that change a designed outcome and not merely an accidental thing that happens to us. I'm trying to make something that we can actually produce together and use as a guide for a transformation to a better world.

Gjoko Muratovski: This has been a topic of interest for you for a long time now. You already had one book called *Massive Change* some years ago. Now *MC24* comes as a follow-up. What has changed in the meantime? What was your motivation and inspiration for writing this book right now?

Design in the Age of Change

Bruce Mau: *Massive Change* was published in 2004, but the book actually started as a design exhibition first. The exhibit took place in Vancouver and then went to Toronto and Chicago. We got an incredible response. We broke attendance records in both Vancouver and Chicago. We beat exhibits of Warhol and Picasso with a design exhibition. At the end of the exhibit, we provided an opportunity for the visitors to provide us with comments. Something that really stuck with me was what people said at the end. They said, "I'm excited. I love this. I'm on your team. I know I want to do this. But how do I do it?" And I realized then that we didn't really know how to explain to people how to do this. We didn't really have a method to share, except our own studio method.

About 10 years ago, the Royal Society of Arts made me an Honorary Royal Designer for Industry. As a part of that, they sent a group of young design leaders to Chicago to meet with my team and me. I showed them my work and some of the things that we've been doing. And they said, "You are a really weird dude. What kind of designer are you?" And I said, "I'm just a designer, and this is what we do." And they said, "Well, we think of design as being defined by the product."

In other words, a designer is what a designer does. A graphic designer does graphics. An architect does buildings. But I am designing social movements and institutions, cities, and carpets. So, what kind of designer am I? I didn't have an answer to this so I just reiterated, "I'm a designer, and that's the work that I do."

How can we change ... everything?

What they said next caught me by surprise. They said, "Okay, but how do you do these things? You showed us the results, but you didn't really explain to us how you do this work?" And I realized that they were right. I actually didn't know how we do the things that we do in my studio. Our way of work has evolved organically over a period of 25 years. We have been challenged by very perplexing and increasingly complex problems and we just developed our own way to address these problems. We did our work intuitively.

Then, I realized that "I don't know" is not a very good answer to that question. I needed to figure out what the real method is because without guiding principles, you can't maintain a consistent performance. That was the start of the process behind the *MC24* book. By analyzing over 25 years of our work, I wanted to understand what were the concepts that really informed us to establish a new way of working. What does it take to do life-centered design? Our design philosophy is to put life at the center of the work that we do and not humans. I think that the concept of human-centered design has really caused many of the challenges that we are facing now. The problem is that we put people above and before anything else, including the natural world, and the ecologies that sustain us. So, we began to really look at what are the methods and principles that we apply to what we call life-centered design. We ended up with 24 of them. It could have been more; it could have been less. We ended up with 24. And that's really the origin of the book.

Design in the Age of Change

Gjoko Muratovski: This is a really beautiful book. In many ways, it does sum up both your design philosophy and your personal design journey. I really enjoyed reading it. I also remember very well when *Massive Change* came out. I was just a student then, completing my Master's degree, and I heard that your book came out. As I was familiar with your previous work, I rushed to the bookstore and got this book immediately. I eagerly wanted to read it. What I quickly realized was that this was a very unusual design book for its time. It opened up all these themes that really challenged what designers do and what designers should do, and what design could be. This was a really thought-provoking book. Now, many years later, I am very pleased to see that you have decided to demystify and unpack some of these ideas further.

Bruce Mau: When we did *Massive Change*, it was organized around, what we call, design economies. These are the regions of your life that are being designed or redesigned. What I was trying to do at the time was to, in some ways, do for design what Marcel Duchamp had done for art—which is to liberate it from what he called "the tyranny of the eye." For him, art was anything you can think of; it was not constrained to visual things. He really tried to get out of the trap of the visual and open it up to the rest of our sensory experiences, and life in general. And he, quite famously, accomplished that. That hadn't happened in design yet.

Design really was—and I think still mostly is—conceived and practiced as a visual practice. So what we said instead, is to try and organize design around economies in which we live and the regions that are changing your life. And I think that it is such an important distinction to say that we live within a designed economy. I mean, imagine the number of times that you can close your eyes and open them in a space where you only see the natural world. You realize that it's practically zero. Even the few times when that is happening, you're actually in a place designed for you to have a natural experience.

For example, think about national parks. National parks aren't natural. If you went into a natural national park, it would kill you. [Laughs] But you want to go and have a good time, be safe, and have a lovely picnic. That's a designed experience. And the same is the case for the market economy, the information economy, the movement economy, and the energy economy. These are economies that are designed and we live within them. Therefore, the quality of design is our quality of life. If, let's say, we have a poor design in the economy of energy, we will have poor performance and, as a result, poor quality of life. The fact that one kind of dimension of the economy of energy is clogging our climate and destroying our quality of life is a design problem, and we designed it that way.

Today we burn about a cubic mile of oil every year. Imagine taking a cubic mile—that's a mile square and a mile high—and setting it on fire. That's what we do every year. But this process has become "invisible" and we don't really see it. Understanding this as a design economy has really led us to a way of thinking about design that was radically different than how we thought about it in the past.

Gjoko Muratovski: Designers today need to be far more accountable for the work that they do than their predecessors. We need to understand the implications of our work, and we need to take responsibility for our actions. In many ways, we need to undo the legacy of our own field. We really need to break our "old habits" and start doing things differently.

Bruce Mau: Yes. I think the most important dimension of this, and the main reason we did the *MC24*, is our argument that we must take responsibility for our designs. When I did *Massive Change*, a lot of people said, "Bruce, you're a megalomaniac, you just want to control everything and you want to design everything." But this is not about control. My preference is actually to do nothing. But if you do something, then you should do this responsibly. So, what is our real responsibility as a society? In the world that we live in, our real responsibility is to design. And when we fail to design, we design for failure. And all over the world, when we don't design our ecology, we destroy it.

What we're doing now is really about going back to places that we did destroy and trying to re-conceive them again as ecologies. But in this process, we're pushing these places to a higher order of complexity. We design not only the ecology of these places but also their infrastructure and amenities. And when you take this approach you have much more challenging and more difficult design responsibilities.

Gjoko Muratovski: Historically speaking, designers have been a part of the problem in so many ways. Over-consumption, planned obsolescence, and waste generation are some of the things that come first to my mind. In part, this has been due to the limitations of design education and a lack of critical thinking skills in the designers' toolkit. This is why we need to educate designers very differently today. That's what I believe. How do you think that we can inspire a new generation of design leaders to create positive change?

Bruce Mau: That's a great question. If you look at the *MC24* principles, the first one is "Inspire." Design is leadership. We need to lead by design. In other words, our responsibility as designers is to inspire. And we have to take that responsibility seriously. I don't wait for hope or inspiration; I take responsibility for producing them. My first impulse is to figure out what will inspire people to change. The question that I ask myself is, "How can I invite people into a new world, and really show them that world?"

I don't think designers really understand how powerful they are—in a political sense of being able to express a new world; to imagine a new world and visualize it. To envision something is to be visual, and designers have the capacity to do that. This is the one common denominator that connects all designers. We're all envisioning a future. We're all imagining, no matter how banal this future may be. Even the worst designers are producing a future. [Laughs] Understanding that we have responsibility for that future, and that we have to begin to understand what the real implications of this future are, is really central to this new way of working that we call life-centered design.

Gjoko Muratovski: Can you share with me an example of how you managed to inspire designers to do better?

Bruce Mau: Once—and I did this quite by accident— I wrote a little manifesto called *The Incomplete Manifesto for Growth*. My wife's sister was really pestering me to contribute to a little magazine that she was doing. I was trying to avoid doing this as much as possible, but she was just unrelenting. So, finally, I said to her that I would do it. At the time, there was something going on in my own practice. I was kind of looking at how to sustain a creative life in the long term. You know, it's easy to be a hot designer for a season but to really lead a creative life is hard. There are a lot of forces that are working against that. So, how do you sustain it? With that in mind, I wrote *The Incomplete Manifesto for Growth*, which I submitted to her magazine. And this manifesto had a really surprising uptake. It's been used in hundreds of courses and classes and translated into dozens of languages. This is when I realized that having a manifesto could be a really powerful technique.

Now we do this for almost all our projects. This is what gives us a direction to follow. A manifesto is very

64

different than a project brief. And you know, when you think about project briefs and design, there has always been a tendency to keep the design briefs short and tight. Everyone wants to have a tight brief; reduced as much as possible. So we went in the opposite direction. We said that we should think of the brief in as complex and difficult way as we can. Rather than focusing on the design object as a discrete entity—a means to an end—we follow the idea that every object is composed of other things and is incorporated into higher-level systems. The direction that we follow is to try and understand that object first. If we are going to make an object of some kind, we first try to understand this object in terms of how this object becomes, what it consumes, and then what are the implications for the larger ecosystem where this product resides.

Gjoko Muratovski: I like thinking in those terms. I also enjoy the complexity of design that most people do not see. By the way, I find it very interesting that you have actually chosen the concept of the manifesto as a platform to communicate your ideas. That is not very common in the design world, but, historically speaking, manifestos have been very powerful tools for inspiring change.

Bruce Mau: After the success of the *Incomplete Manifesto*, we started using this concept in our workshops. In the beginning, we asked people to do a six-minute manifesto. The experience of doing this was so powerful that often—almost always—someone, or more people, were crying. Then we reduced the exercise to a three-minute manifesto because we saw that people actually finished their manifestos early. We realized that people actually know what they want in their life. Then this became something that we almost always do with our projects and at our workshops or with clients. We found this to be a very effective way of articulating an ambition that can be shared as a collective commitment.

We also wrote a manifesto for Freeman, the company where I work as a Chief Design Officer. We wrote the Freeman manifesto together as a group. And the manifesto really articulates our vision for the future of the company. Our responsibility to the community, to the people that we serve, and the people we employ. This really is a way of articulating our highest purpose and our highest ambition as a design goal that we can then break down into pieces and execute the pieces.

Gjoko Muratovski: Bruce, how would you approach the design for the "new normal" that we are experiencing today?

Bruce Mau: The "new normal" for me today is all about shifting our perspective. If we say, as designers, that the real design problem is to design the "new normal," then this fundamentally changes our approach. If we want to introduce a sustainable way of life, then this should be the life for radicals, pioneers, and heroic champions. If we do that, then we will be doomed. What we need to do is to make this way of life not hard, not difficult, and not challenging. We have to make it the easiest, the most fun, exciting, and sexy thing to do. We need to make this way of life beautiful.

However, I find it really fascinating that we have almost no discussion of beauty in the design profession. If I was an architecture student and I walked into an architecture school today, and I put up my project and I said, "I did it because it's beautiful," I will get a Fail. [Laughs] And I think that's a real shortcoming in our imagination because there are a million forms of beauty. Yes, the concept of beauty is always shifting culturally. We think of beauty differently in different places and cultures. But the common denominator is that beauty is the highest form of cultural attainment. We will spend more for beauty. We will go the distance. We will suffer pain for beauty. What we will do for beauty is really unlimited, and yet, we don't really think of beauty as a guiding principle. This is why I talk to my clients about having a beauty strategy. I ask them, "What is your beauty strategy?"

Most companies have no concept for this. But a company like Apple was built on a beauty strategy. Steve Jobs decided to put beauty into Apple's products—to the extent that he rejected motherboards that didn't look good. He would look at a motherboard, which is a purely technical thing—an arrangement of objects to perform functions—and he would say, "This is not beautiful, take it back." He wanted beauty and order in the very essence of the product. Now, if you take Apple today and you took the beauty out of it, you'd have a reasonably good technology company. But with the beauty that their products embody, you have a company worth $2 trillion—the most valuable company in the history of humankind. This is why I don't understand why business leaders everywhere don't realize that beauty is an effective competitive idea.

Gjoko Muratovski: I think it's because the notion of beauty can be very subjective. Otherwise, you're very correct. There is a constant pursuit of beauty in all cultures. From a Western point of view, if we take the periods of Classical Antiquity and the Renaissance, we can see that they have been obsessed with the pursuit of beauty. But we also know that beauty is a construct that changes over time. And even within the same culture, beauty can take different shapes and different forms as social norms change and differ from group-to-group. As a result, it is a very difficult thing to objectively determine what beauty is. What beauty is for Steve Jobs is one thing; for his engineers, beauty is a completely different thing. Those who are in the position of power to decide what beauty is, is what beauty becomes. And this is a very interesting thing about our society.

Bruce Mau: Well, if you think about, like what Buckminster Fuller said, "I don't really think about beauty very much, but I know that if the result isn't beautiful, it's probably not right." There's a kind of order and truth in beauty that we can't precisely quantify. But what we can do is say, "There are dimensions of beauty," and that's what we've done in *MC24*. There are thirteen dimensions of beauty that you can understand and integrate into your thinking and apply in your work.

How can we change ... everything?

Gjoko Muratovski: I think that the relationship between beauty and practicality is an interesting one. In a way, some things are beautiful because they're easy to use, they're simple, and they're very streamlined. But in some cases, the beauty comes at the cost of function. And one perfect example of this is Philippe Starck's lemon juicer for Alessi. [Gjoko picks up the juicer from the bookshelf behind him.]

Bruce Mau: Useless. [Laughs]

Gjoko Muratovski: Useless, but exceptionally beautiful, right? [Laughs] Nevertheless, it is a design icon!

Bruce Mau: If you want to sponsor a flawed design, then yes—you can consider this to be an absolute design icon.

Gjoko Muratovski: That's true, and this is the confusing and contradictory message that the field of design so often projects. The fact is that this object is widely recognized as a design icon because it's beautiful. However, the paradox is that if a design student, let's say one of ours, designs something like this then we will have to fail the student, by default—simply because the student has designed a product that is impractical and flawed on multiple levels. Such a product disregards all notions of what product design is all about. But there is no doubt that this particular product is a beautiful object. And by the way, this product is so useless that I have never used it in a kitchen. It only sits on the shelf here in my office for my amusement.

69

Design in the Age of Change

Bruce Mau: I would like to show you a beauty of a different kind and on an extraordinary scale. This is the skeleton of one sea creature. [Bruce picks up a small and very intricate skeleton from his desk.] This creature has a skeleton made of glass. Can you see how crazy-beautiful this is?

Gjoko Muratovski: This is incredible! I've never seen anything like this.

Bruce Mau: Nature doesn't do things like we do. Nature can grow things in the most interesting ways. This skeleton has such a beautiful intelligence in its conception that is powerful and really undeniable. It is visually beautiful, too. And this is a good lesson for us. In the future, we will need to learn how to grow the things that we need and want, because this is how life works. We need to use the billions of years of design intelligence that is built into our natural world, learn from it, and make this knowledge accessible to designers everywhere.

Gjoko Muratovski: Bruce, let's expand the topic of our conversation further. Can you also share with me an example of a successful social change project that you have designed and led?

Bruce Mau: Well, one of my favorite things I've ever been involved in is a project called GuateAmala. This project started with a letter from the Minister of Education of Guatemala. She wrote me a letter, and in

the letter, she basically explained that she was
part of a group of citizens who were working to
imagine a better future for Guatemala. Their research
and work had led them to me and they'd be interested
in talking to me about being part of this project. The
letter, however, arrived with no return address or
phone number. I guess in Guatemala everyone knows
how to get in touch with the Minister of Education.
[Laughs]

I told my assistant that, no doubt, these folks are
going to try to contact us again, so please get in touch
with me wherever I am. So, a few days later, they did.
We talked and they explained to me that they had
36 years of civil war. As a result, they felt that their
people had lost the ability to "dream." I could hardly
imagine that an ability to "dream" could be lost, but,
obviously, I have not lived through 36 years of civil
war. Then, they explained to me that during that time,
the future for their people was wiped out. The idea of
thinking about the future was practically eliminated
and was replaced with the notion of thinking about
survival, now and today. "When we talk to our kids
and ask them what they want to be when they grow
up, they don't have an answer," they said, "They don't
think they will grow up. At least this is not a part of
their kind of imagination." And so, they asked me if
we could help them.

A few days later—and this happened very, very
quickly—we were on our way to Guatemala. As soon
as we arrived, they took me to meet the Vice President
of Guatemala. And they said, "This is Bruce, and

71

he's going to redesign Guatemala." [Laughs] And
I said,

No, No, No, I never said anything like that, and I'm
not going do that. You are going to do it. You are the
ones who are going to redesign Guatemala. I will help
you apply design to the problem, I can give you the
strategic tools and methods that you will need, and
I can accelerate your work. But in the end, it's going to
be you who will do this. If anyone who isn't
Guatemalan offers you to do that on your behalf, you
should run away from them.

And so they said, "Okay, then, we want you to help
us change the name of the country." Wow! [Laughs]
"You guys are really big thinkers. Why would you
want to do that?" And they explained to me that the
Indigenous people have called this place Guate. When
the Spanish arrived, they hated the place, so they named
it *GuateMala*. In Spanish, this means "bad Guate." So,
they said, "How would you like to live in the United
States of a Bad Place?" They really got a point there.
I mean, maybe this was something that we should really
think about. We started thinking about this, and in the
process, we added an extra "a" to the name to become
GuateAmala. This means, "love of Guate." This is how
the movement started. Our design project was really
to design the *Amala* movement and to build, what we
called, the foundations of life.

They had 36 years of culture of death, and we now
wanted to build a culture of life. But you can't simply

turn off death and turn on life. We met with a woman who saw every male in her extended family killed just before the end of the war. This was the case in many of the communities that we've met. This was so traumatic for them that they couldn't even talk about it among themselves. Then we realized that these experiences are now embedded in their culture. If they are to build a culture of life, it will take years and decades of work to invest in creating this new culture and figuring out what that means in this context. I think that this project really shows that design can have an impact on a dramatic scale. For me, this was one of the best things that I've done in my life. In the coming months, we will start working on the next phase of this project.

Gjoko Muratovski: This is a very noble project. Very few designers can say that they have been in a position to inspire a change on such a large scale, and in such a meaningful and engaging way. How many people on your team worked with you on that?

Bruce Mau: Oh, it was actually a small group. It was only four or five people from our end, but a very big group of Guatemalan locals got involved. From our end, we were really working on strategy, communication, and designing the foundation of the project, while they were focused on the project execution.

Our goal at the time was to get 1000 volunteers. We thought if we could have 1000 people committed to the movement, we could really make an impact. By the end of it, we had over 20,000 people who signed up as volunteers. And this is in a country where for the last 36 years, if you sign your name on things, a black SUV would show up and you would never be seen again. To see so many people from Guatemala making a public commitment to join a movement for social justice was a really profound experience, for me.

Gjoko Muratovski: Thank you so much for sharing this very inspiring example, Bruce. What would be your advice for any homegrown design activists; for individuals who want to create movements in places without government support or without the possibility of securing funding? How can design activists initiate grassroots movements, such as the one that you were helping to create in Guatemala?

Bruce Mau: I think that it's never been more possible to participate in change. I think that the connectedness that we have today can allow us to join forces and overcome some of the most vexing problems that humankind has ever faced. Now, sadly, as we've seen recently—in the United States especially—we can also use that connectedness to gather against things that are positive for our society. I think that there is an urgency now for designers to use their "superpowers" to inspire people to gather for positive things—for an equitable world, a sustainable world, for access to education, and new possibilities.

How can we change ... everything?

Gjoko Muratovski: Bruce, thank you so much for sharing your ideas with me. You've had a remarkable career, and I really enjoyed learning more about your design philosophy and professional experiences.

Bruce Mau: So far, so good, Gjoko. Yet, I still feel like I'm just getting started. [Laughs] Thank you for having me as a guest. I enjoyed our conversation.

What is the political power of design?
In conversation with Steven Heller

Over the last few years, and, in 2020, in particular, we have seen a surge in protests, civil unrest, and activism. Just a year prior, a new generation of climate activists took the world by a storm. Youth-led global climate strikes, led by the then 16-year-old Greta Thunberg, took epic proportions. The only reason why these protests were somewhat curbed in 2020 was due to the COVID-19 social distancing limitations. However, the pandemic didn't put a stop to many other protests that took place in 2020. The Black Lives Matter protests in the United States were reignited after the police killing of George Floyd in Minneapolis. This civil rights movement quickly spread across the country and overseas where other Black minority populations, who protested in the context of their own colonial legacies, adopted it. In anticipation of the Black Friday shopping event, thousands of Amazon warehouse workers from around the world went on strike and staged protests against the working conditions provided to them by "the world's most valuable company."

Others, however, decided to protest the "stay-at-home" orders that were issued by many countries in an attempt to curb down the spread of the pandemic. Then, in the very first days of 2021, the United States were shocked in the wake of the Washington, DC, riot where a mob of Donald Trump supporters stormed the United States Capitol building in an attempt to overturn his defeat in the 2020 presidential elections. And this is just a small sample of the various forms of activism that we have witnessed during this brief period.

Designers, like most people, are not indifferent to various forms of activism. This is something that I often see even within our student population who can be quite vocal at times and not afraid to stand up for the things that they believe in. In 2020, one of our recent graduates—Julia Bond—confronted Adidas for the racists' remarks that she faced there after being hired as a junior designer. Her protest was soon joined in solidarity by hundreds of other Adidas employees and was covered by *The New York Times* on more than one occasion. Her convictions were so strong that she continued her protest even after the Global Head of Human Resources resigned and after Adidas pledged to support a number of initiatives to address the representation of racial disparity. What she really wanted was a genuine apology and a public acknowledgment by the brand in their complicity in systemic racism.

One person who studied in great depth the role of activism in the field of design, and the effect that design activists have on the world, is Steven Heller. Chances are that even if you are vaguely interested in design,

What is the political power of design?

you have probably come across some of Steven's books on design. As an author and editor, Steven has published approximately two hundred books on design and contributed to hundreds of other design publications. As a design critic, he has documented and reflected on the history and practice of design with incredible depth, breadth, and scope. For more than 30 years, he was an Art Director for *The New York Times* and writer for *The New York Times Book Review*. He is also the recipient of several highly prestigious awards, including the AIGA's Medal for Lifetime Achievement Award, the Art Directors Club Hall of Fame Award, and the National Design Award, which was presented to him at a White House ceremony by the First Lady of the United States at the time, Michelle Obama.

Gjoko Muratovski: I have always been interested in the political side of design—from the way the design has been used by various governments or regimes, to how it is used by various civic movements. More than a decade ago, as the Director of the Greenpeace Design Awards, I helped Greenpeace establish a global design competition aimed to attract design activists who could help the organization develop new campaigns. This was a very successful program that attracted over 1500 designers from 77 countries. It was amazing to see how passionate the global design community is when it comes to supporting social and environmental causes. Your book *Citizen Designer* is based on this sentiment. What was your interest in studying this topic?

Design in the Age of Change

Steven Heller: Well, I've been politicized since I was a kid, growing up in New York City. I come from a family with liberal beliefs. I had an uncle who was a Columbia University professor and he was quite political. He introduced me to the ideas of liberalism, socialism, and communism; civil rights as well. This was an important issue and it still is.

The civil rights movement was just beginning to come to the fore when I was 8 or 9 years old. I got a pretty good education from my uncle on this, and I wanted to figure out how to translate it. So I translated it through politics. First, when I was 10 years old I volunteered for John F. Kennedy. I got to meet him even. Then, when I was older—about 15 years old—I started working for underground, leftwing newspapers in New York. I did that for a number of years before moving on to *The New York Times.* This is what put me in the community of activism.

About twenty years ago, designers who were of the previous generation than mine had been very active in political terms. They were not just making designs or marching in parades. They were actually helping people on a macro and micro level. I felt that designers of my day needed a kick in the butt. This is how the book came about.

The idea behind the first edition of *Citizen Designer,* which I did with Veronique Vienne—who's a design writer living in Paris—was to gather together people's thoughts on what activism, politics, and social consciousness were all about. We published the book at a time when more and more people were working with the poor to bring them

80

into greater educational opportunities. For those people, the design was seen not only as a way of bringing people into the mainstream but into a counterculture, as well. In response, we introduced the term "citizen designer" as an overall umbrella term for any designer who had a tendency or a penchant for social impact.

Gjoko Muratovski: Can you unpack the idea of "citizen designer" further?

Steven Heller: Well, the term basically comes from something Milton Glaser had said to me—I knew Milton for decades. In fact, the new edition of *Citizen Designer* was, in a way, dedicated to him by publishing one of his essays on "what does it mean being a good citizen?" He was the one that said to me at lunch one day years ago, that designers couldn't just be slaves to their clients. "They can't just do what a client wants, without introspection or circumspection. Designers need to be good citizens." That's the most you can ask of anybody. And what does citizenship mean? Citizenship means caring for others. It means taking responsibility for your own actions. It means as he puts it, to do no harm. And so I globed on to that word "citizen." And "citizen designer" seemed like the logical extension for our field.

Gjoko Muratovski: It's interesting to hear how this inspiration comes from Milton Glaser—the designer behind the "I Love NY" logo—who sadly passed just recently [on June 26, 2020]. What a great loss to the design community.

Milton and you were good friends, and I think that you both shared a very similar ideological background growing up. He was also, I believe, quite inspired by similar things like you when he was a child. He also came from a family background where activism was a normal thing.

Steven Heller: Activism was expected of him. He was from the Bronx. I was born in Manhattan. His family were immigrants from Hungary. Milton was born at the time of great social flux, the Great Depression. He lived in something called the Coops, which was a worker's housing project in the Bronx. He got radicalized as a kid by seeing things such as rent strikes and seeing police on horses breaking up those rent strikes. He even had a photograph from one of those riots that he showed when we did a talk together at Cooper Union.

He's always been on the front line of social activism. For some people, the term "social activism" is a buzzword that they use to enter into a particular social group. But Milton always put his money where his mouth was, and he put his design where his mind was. He always did things that he—rightly or wrongly—thought would be of benefit to the community and the world at large.

Gjoko Muratovski: He did a lovely book on the topic of dissent with Mirko Ilić—*Design of Dissent.*

Steven Heller: For *Design of Dissent,* Mirko and Milton researched hundreds of posters that were being done for

82

different political reasons and movements. The book was done in two editions.

Gjoko Muratovski: Yeah, I have the latest edition. It's a pretty good collection of different types of political campaigns. It complements your book well, by the way. So, you published the first edition of *Citizen Designer* in 2003, and the second one in 2018. What has changed on the design scene in this area in the fifteen years between the two editions?

Steven Heller: Well, there has been more active participation in this area by organizations such as Greenpeace, in terms of environmental activism, and also in social, guerrilla activism.

Overall, the field has gotten more professional. Since the introduction of the computer, design as a field has taken on both mainstream and experimental veneers, and, as a result, there are now more graphic designers than ever before. Whenever there's an issue that needs to be addressed, you'll find two or three people sending out calls for entry to make posters. I have mixed feelings about all that but I think there is a considerable concern in the world; even more so since the US Presidential election of 2016 when Donald Trump won. There is a widespread sense that we are losing our freedoms and we are losing our planet to the greedy upper class.

In the time between the first edition and the second edition, people have caught on to the fact that we may be going to hell, and they need to do something. I think there's a lot more activity that has happened naturally

by coming out of the George W. Bush administration
and its unnecessary wars. Barack Obama's presidency
was very much predicated on changing the world, even
though that didn't continue. Donald Trump is all about
destroying the world, and he had a very good opportunity to do that.

Gjoko Muratovski: Do you think designers can be influential enough with their work to ascertain positive conversations in the current political discourse?

Steven Heller: I think that we used to think of designers
as a segmented group of aesthetes or exceptional people
that could work with one foot in the realm of art and
aesthetics, and the other foot in the world of commerce
and pragmatics. I think that designers have now come
together. Design is no longer about pure commerce and
it's no longer about pure aestheticism. It's a tool, and it's
a profession that requires you to have the skills and the
tools. For example, I think that there is enough sophisti-
cation today for us to have an Art Director in the White
House. In fact, Obama did have this with Ashleigh Axios
in the role. Many things changed when Obama was
president. This period that we now call the Obama Era
brought a big change to the ways in which design was
seen by the government.

Gjoko Muratovski: Interesting. I think that probably
the biggest achievement of the Obama administration
was the establishment of the White House Presidential
Innovations Fellows Program where many designers

were brought in, alongside innovators and entrepreneurs, into the federal government to drive innovation. I was involved at some point with that particular program as an advisor. I found it very inspiring that designers were given such a voice and were enabled to instigate positive change.

But you know, the most important contribution to the field of design by an American president actually came from Nixon, as funny as that may sound.

Steven Heller: Yes, Richard Nixon. That is the last person that we could expect to have actually contributed so much to the design culture of the United States. He started the National Endowment for the Arts and he started the Federal Design Program. I think he did that because he didn't know anything about it. Clearly, he had an advisor, or advisors, who said this is a good thing to do. He didn't have a political agenda related to design so it just happened.

Gjoko Muratovski: It was incredible, really. It was all about pure design and pure architecture, without politics. And in many ways, the legacy of this program still lives on, even today.

Steven Heller: Yeah, Milton Glaser and I were on a government panel during the Clinton administration to judge the Federal Design Awards. We were amused because, on the one hand, there were the ultra-professional architects and graphic designers doing things for the Parks Department, various federal buildings, the

Design in the Age of Change

United States Post Office. And then, on the other hand, you could find amateur design events and projects placed alongside this. All of this was put together under this umbrella of federal design projects. There wasn't a single person who was in charge of it. Everything was very democratic.

Gjoko Muratovski: You know, just recently, I uncovered some actual original documents for the design programs from the federal government, from the time of Nixon. I have them here in my office, actually. These documents are about design conferences that the government was hosting so that they could better understand design and architecture. Reading the conference program is like reading a "who's who" in design and architecture in the United States at the time. It was incredible seeing that. I think that this was probably the greatest time for design in American history, in terms of how much designers were empowered to just be themselves.

Steven Heller: Yeah, it was kind of a crazy anomaly. All of that design work became an important part of the American culture. Clearly, they understood at the time that design could be an exceptionally effective tool for communication, propaganda, and persuasion.

Gjoko Muratovski: This is a very interesting example of how the power of design and architecture has been used for public good and politics. We both know many, many examples in history where that has been done with the opposite intent.

86

What is the political power of design?

Steven Heller: Well, it also goes back to ancient times where the pharaohs created the pyramids and the Sphinx. And those were ostensibly political acts, using the design that has been indelible in our minds for ages. I did a book called *Iron Fists: Branding the 20th-Century Totalitarian State*, where I examined such things in more detail.

Gjoko Muratovski: Yep. I have it here in my personal library. By the way, did you know that the largest pyramids were actually built by the weakest Egyptian dynasty? The extravagance of the Cheops pyramid was nothing more than an illusionary display of power. Egyptian dynasties that followed the Cheops dynasty were far more powerful, yet they dramatically reduced the scale of their pyramids. Instead, they invested their resources in other ways: launching long-distance trading expeditions, military campaigns of conquest, maintaining big garrisons, constructing fortresses, irrigation works, and ship channels—all of which were far beyond the capabilities of Cheops. In the case of the Cheops dynasty, the construction of the largest building in the world—and, for over 40 centuries, the tallest—was nothing more than a form of architectural propaganda meant to deify the ruling class and hide their absence of real power.

Steven Heller: One interesting thing about the design of power and the design of fear are decorations—military decorations, especially. For example, look at North Korea. It's amazing that their officers are just covered with emblems and medals. Each one has some significance, of course. But the larger significance, from a design standpoint, is to show that they're preeminent. Whereas, their leader wears nothing but a black Nehru jacket, or a simple Mao jacket, and this creates quite the contrast.

Gjoko Muratovski: That idea of playing with contrast in terms of power is quite interesting. In fact, Hitler was doing that quite well. He had specially designed uniforms for his officers, which were in a very similar way, covered with medals and gold braids—all very theatrical, of course—while he wore a very simple gray uniform with only one medal, the Iron Cross. He believed that by creating such a stark contrast between himself and his subordinates would make him appear even more powerful. That was a very clever visual strategy.

Steven Heller: When you want to show that you're powerful and you want to show that you have control of something, you add to yourself. You can add decorations, you surround yourself with symbols of power, or you add adjectives such as Your Honor, Your Eminence, or Your Royal Highness. That's why America, even though it has a very flawed origin story, is in its pure democratic sense kind of fascinating because we don't have those over-illustrious titles. And I think that was done by design.

Gjoko Muratovski: I agree. Everything leading to the independence of America and its subsequent manifestations of soveregnity was by design. That in itself is a fascinating story. But let's circle back to the topic of activism ...

What is the political power of design?

When some people engage in such activities, they do that at a great personal sacrifice. Their personal beliefs and convictions are often greater than the price that they sometimes have to pay for their actions. Making a stand for these activists is often the last resort. Other people, however, engage in such activities because they have the social and financial stability that allows them to do that. In other words, they do that because they can afford to. To what degree do you think privilege plays a role in activism?

Steven Heller: I think that privilege plays a large role. I was very active during the 1960s anti-war movement, working for publications, working for groups and organizations, marching for other reasons. I was arrested and jailed twice, but I never felt threatened. I wasn't feeling like African Americans feel today. If they go out in the street and demonstrate they could actually get a bullet in them, or have their neck broken.

My parents were liberal New Yorkers, but they didn't agree with me when I was protesting the Vietnam War because they were also Depression children who believed that Franklin D. Roosevelt was a saint, and, therefore, by proxy, the United States was saintly. So we got into some generational arguments, but I still was able to maintain my position and ability to be active because my parents could afford to allow me that license. I think that many kids of wealthy parents, going back decades, may be even a century, were able to be active because they had the silver spoon in their mouth. I think that privilege has a lot to do with how you ultimately relate to the world.

Design in the Age of Change

Gjoko Muratovski: Privilege allows people the ability to express themselves—politically and creatively. Of course, neither politics nor creativity is exclusive to privileged people, but the path to pursuing both is easier when you come from a privileged background. This is something that I have come across often in the university environment as well. Take, for example, studying subjects like design, art, and architecture—or subjects related to humanities in general. Enrolling in subjects like these is often a very privileged thing to do because it comes down to not only whether you can afford to study such subjects but it also comes down to your upbringing. When you were a child and then a teenager, did your parents encourage you, or let's say, tolerated you when expressing yourself or engaging in creative activities? Were they financially affluent enough to afford you doing this? Did you feel comfortable enough at home to do this? I know that there are exceptions to this, but the socio-economic background from which a person comes has a lot to do with the path they chose to pursue in life.

For example, when somebody decides to become a designer, or an artist, or an activist, this is usually because they feel comfortable enough to do that. I often find that many design activists do this because they can. They're in a position of privilege to afford to do it. We both know that this kind of work is done pro bono. You don't really make money by being an activist. Activism is an altruistic act. So, when you need to make a choice between doing a commissioned work versus doing a pro bono project, you really need to feel comfortable to select the latter.

What is the political power of design?

Steven Heller: Well, if you have to choose, you choose to pay the rent. But a lot of people don't make the choice. They just do both. They can have their cake and eat it, and there's nothing wrong with that. If you can work in a commercial capacity and earn a living, but spend your passionate hours doing what you are impassioned by, then good luck—do it.

Gjoko Muratovski: Many advertising agencies produce activist campaigns simply because this has often been seen in the industry as an easy way to attract awards and gain public attention to their work. Since these campaigns are often done pro bono, the agencies retain usually all creative control over the ads. This, in return, means that they can push the creative envelope much further than they can with paying clients. But I think that there is rarely a real intent in changing anything with these campaigns. Outside of serving as vanity projects, do you find that these campaigns are at all effective?

Steven Heller: Well, it really depends on the campaign. I've seen many birth control, pro-abortion public service announcements that are very powerful and very useful. I see Ben & Jerry's as having raised the consciousness of many people through their campaigns, and by the transparency on their packages when Ben & Jerry's Ice Cream was owned by Ben & Jerry. Unilever owns them now. Kenneth Cole gives a fair amount of his profits to significant charities. The Bill & Melinda Gates Foundation has really made great strides in the areas that they've supported. Sometimes these things work well. If you look at the turn of the twentieth century, the Gilded Age, it was the Carnegies, J.P. Morgan, Goulds, Rockefellers, and other billionaires in America that started the major philanthropies. None of these people, I would say, would stand up to the test of time as righteous people, but they did righteous things.

Gjoko Muratovski: These people established their philanthropies as a part of their public relations campaigns because they had such bad publicity surrounding them. They were advised to do these things in order to create a better image for themselves. Take, for example, Alfred Nobel and the Nobel Prize. Most people are not aware that he made his fortune as an arms dealer and developer of weapon technologies. Ironically, he established an international prize for peace in his name as a way to cleanse his legacy.

Steven Heller: Yeah, I mean, Nobel invented dynamite and other powerful explosives. But, you can hate the messenger and love the message. Ultimately, their foundations, their charities, and their philanthropy have done a lot of good for many people.

Gjoko Muratovski: I guess you are right. I mean, there is certainly something good coming out of it now, but the original intent was for this to be simply a PR exercise.

Steven Heller: Well, it's normal for them to respond to the public opinion, just as you and I respond to the opinion of our peers. It's great that these things are happening if they serve a positive purpose.

What is the political power of design?

Gjoko Muratovski: What do you think it takes for an activist campaign to truly resonate with people?

Steven Heller: What it takes is honesty. It needs to look good. And it has to be promoting a solid message. You also need to be very clear on whom your audience is, what your audience wants, and what you want to give the audience. This is what it takes for a successful activist campaign.

Gjoko Muratovski: I find that designers today are becoming increasingly socially aware and increasingly political, in a sense that they seek to pursue greater meaning in the work that they do. I believe that young designers today feel more empowered, more responsible, and more accountable for the work that they do. But at the same time, they also like to hold accountable their employers, the government, and the society at large.

Steven Heller: As they should.

Gjoko Muratovski: I see a very strong spirit of social justice with the new generation of designers that are coming forward. What would you recommend to young, emerging designers who are interested in grassroots activism?

Steven Heller: I'd recommend that they find groups to work with and learn all they can about what that particular group or individual or organization needs and wants. The great thing that a designer is able to do now is to help these groups strategize. It's not just about making a logo. It's not just about making a poster. It's what does that logo and poster do as a supplement to the overall message. And I think young designers should find real-world ways of doing that.

I'm teaching a class in propaganda—the good and the bad of propaganda. And it's a history class. But at the same time, it's a studio class where I teach these students how to figure out what is important for them in their own lives, and in their own countries—because we have so many foreign students at the School of Visual Arts in New York. I ask them to think about what is it that they would want to change by using their talents and skills, and then I ask them to create a campaign for that. Sometimes, their work leads to extraordinary results. For example, the Umbrella Movement—the yellow umbrella protests in Hong Kong—was created by one of our Chinese students and this campaign became known around the world. I was his first convert.

Gjoko Muratovski: There are many interesting examples of this type of activism and movements around the world. One particularly interesting movement was organized against Slobodan Milošević, the last president of Yugoslavia. The movement that helped overthrow Milošević was launched by an organization called *Otpor*, which means "resistance" in Serbian. Their logo featured a clenched fist, a typical symbol indicating resistance. What makes this particularly interesting is that this was the first time that—in that part of the world—that we got "branded" revolutions. Then, a string of other branded revolutions in the region followed. They were known as

What is the political power of design?

The Color Revolutions. Then, we witnessed The Arab Spring—another string of branded revolutions in North Africa and the Middle East. It became evident that these kinds of revolutions were conceived in America because this type of quasi-commercial branding was simply not typical to the local cultures there. This was very much an imported form of propaganda. It takes a very different mindset conceiving such campaigns. These kinds of campaigns, the Umbrella Movement included, do not just spontaneously appear; they are specially designed by someone. And as I just learned, sometimes people learn how to do these things in your classes. I find that to be pretty amazing.

Steven Heller: Gjoko, this has been a great conversation. Thank you so much. I very much enjoyed talking with you and it's really a pleasure. I wish we could do this more often, to be honest.

Gjoko Muratovski: So do I, Steve. Hope to see you in New York City, next time.

Why do we fear gender-neutrality?
In conversation with Alok Vaid-Menon

Gender neutrality is a topic of conversation that is now starting to emerge in the mainstream of our society. Gender-neutral pronouns such as "they/them/their" are now widely and formally accepted in a singular form. Furthermore, a whole new movement of gender-free clothing is now taking place in the fashion world, with brands such as Gucci, Kenzo, and Louis Vuitton currently leading the way. Yet, despite the glamorous overture of the fashion world and the institutionalization of gender-neutral pronouns, this topic is still a very sensitive social issue. In fact, this topic hides much bigger issues than most people understand. The lack of discussions surrounding gender neutrality causes ignorance, as well as lack of empathy and compassion. In return, this also leads to violence. This is why I believe that this is an issue that needs to be discussed more often and more openly, and my guest for this topic is Alok Vaid-Menon.

Alok is a highly prominent figure of the gender non-conforming movement. They are a gender non-conforming activist, writer, poet, fashion designer, and performance artist, widely recognized for their distinctive style. As a mixed-media artist, Alok explores themes of gender, race, trauma, belonging, and the human condition. They are a very passionate advocate for issues related to gender neutrality, degendering fashion, and the challenges that the trans and gender non-conforming communities face on a daily basis. Alok is frequently covered by the press and the media—from the PBS News Hour and MTV to *The New Yorker*, *Vogue*, and the HBO documentary, *The Trans List*. With nearly 1 million followers on their Instagram account, there is no doubt that Alok is a very powerful voice for this underrepresented community.

Gjoko Muratovski: Alok, let's start by talking about fashion. Despite some very high-profile endorsements in recent times, the topic of gender-neutral fashion still remains a polarizing issue. Why is this the case?

Alok Vaid-Menon: I think that one thing that is really important for people to understand is that clothing is essentially gender-neutral. Gender neutrality does not just appear when a non-binary fashion designer introduces it in their work, nor does it appear when a fashion collection is marketed as gender-neutral. Clothes are, by definition, gender-neutral. They are inanimate objects and as such, they don't actually have a gender.

I find it confusing when we say "women's clothing" and "men's clothing." Clothes can't think and declare a gender for themselves. The problem is that we are actually recruiting inanimate objects into our socially

Why do we fear gender-neutrality?

constructed ideas of gender. Clothes inherently don't have a gender. In this regard, gender neutrality is not something that is coming in and erasing the notion of gender; it's what already exists before gender is imposed on it. Gender neutrality is the default. Those who oppose gender neutrality often describe this as a force that is coming in to erase or take away gender. But the force that is actually doing that is the notion of gendering.

Gjoko Muratovski: That is a very interesting juxtaposition. Why do you think that we need gender-neutral fashion to become the "new normal?"

Alok Vaid-Menon: It's so great that we're having this conversation today because *Vogue* just released their December 2020 issue, and this is the first time ever that they are having a cis male on the cover—Harry Styles. In all of his portraits, he's actually wearing gowns from Gucci, and gowns from Harry Lambert, which is a stylist that he works with. When I was reading the magazine this morning, I was wowed. This is such a huge moment in contemporary culture. Never did I think that in my lifetime that we'd be able to have someone who identifies as a man, wearing a gown, and being featured like that in American *Vogue*.

I think it's really important to understand how we got to this moment. One of the things that people often don't know in the Western world is that in New York City, which is where I live, it used to be illegal to "cross-dress" from around the 1870s until the 1970s. For an entire century, there were a series of laws called the Masquerade laws, which were prohibiting this kind of behavior. The Masquerade laws essentially required people to wear at least three articles of clothing that are consistent with their assigned sex, otherwise they could be thrown into prison. In the early 1900s, women would be arrested for wearing suits, and men would be arrested for wearing dresses. It was only due to the tireless activism of trans communities—who were continually being arrested and thrown into prison—that those kinds of laws were repealed in the 1970s, after the Stonewall riots. These riots were a series of spontaneous demonstrations by members of the gay community in response to a police raid that began in the early morning hours of June 28, 1969, at the Stonewall Inn in the Greenwich Village neighborhood of Manhattan.

I think that we need to de-gender fashion or have gender-neutral fashion because, first and foremost, this could serve as an anti-violence mechanism. We exist in a world where if people see someone like me—who they perceive as a man wearing articles of clothing that they perceive to be women's clothing—they may respond with violence. Whereas, if we say that anyone can wear a skirt and anyone can wear makeup, we no longer have that same sense of dissonance, and, therefore, the threat of violence will be decreased. My advocacy in this space exists because I'm trying to end gender-based violence.

I would also like to make three points here. First one is that gender-based violence is not only physical violence aimed at transgender and gender-neutral people. Gender-based violence takes place when cis men want to wear pink, and people tell them that's not masculine and that they shouldn't do that. Or, when women don't want to feel the pressure to wear makeup and people call them up on that. These rigid ideas of gender and beauty, and gender and clothing, actually end up harming everyone.

Another point that I would like to make is that fashion should be about creative expression and not about categorization. Fashion is an art form and part of the purpose of art is to blur arbitrary norms and to question and provoke culture. I can argue here that gendering fashion is holding fashion design back because people are more invested in reproducing stereotypes than reproducing beauty. What my favorite fashion designers are doing is actually trying to evolve fashion. Alexander McQueen was a particularly great example of this. Designers would try to reimagine what a silhouette is or reimagine what a shoe should be. How can, otherwise, fashion designers say that they are so creative if they are still dividing people into one of two categories? I find this as an inconsistency in the fashion world because true creativity reveals all categories to be artificial and unambitious.

Then, my third point is that gender neutrality is not a historically new issue. One of the things that I do in my work is research on the history of gender and fashion. What I have determined is that a lot of what we now call "feminine," things like wigs, makeup, heels, leggings, lace, and plume, were actually worn by men for hundreds of years in Europe. So, when we are saying, "gender neutrality," we're just harkening back to what already was. This is not a new thing. This is actually about returning to an old thing.

Design in the Age of Change

Lace and heels, for example, became associated with femininity only after the Age of Enlightenment, once the Industrial Revolution began. This is when we started seeing the introduction of separate spheres for men and women. This is the period in society when men were supposed to be seen as productive workers, while women were supposed to stay at home and take care of domesticity, or to serve as accessories and ornamentalized objects. This is the moment when fashion design shifted. From here on, women were tasked with wearing clothing that could not be worked in, like corsets or gowns, whereas men were expected to wear more functional clothing.

And in line with this, I would like to say that I find the work of the art historian, Anne Hollander, quite interesting. In her studies, she writes that the suit for men actually became a way of emphasizing that men had legs and that they could walk and work. Whereas the gown and the skirt were created to instill a sense of mystery and allure around womanhood; that women could just belong to where men imagined that they should be.

The overarching point that I want to make here is that de-gendering fashion is also a form of resisting sexism and misogyny. We still have these ideas that feminine garb is weak, and masculine garb is strong, that men are agile, rational thinkers, and women are the ridiculous, hyper-excessive, hyper-stylized, and hyper-characterized tropes. But in reality, all of us have both of those attributes in us.

Much of the contention right now, about de-gendering fashion, is misplaced. People like myself are often accused of advancing some kind of novel and disruptive concepts, while, in fact, this idea is actually quite old.

Gjoko Muratovski: Alok, you're absolutely correct when you say that fashion throughout history was not defined in the same way as it is now. You mentioned Europe during the Age of Enlightenment as an example. The French court, especially during the reign of Louis XIV (1643–1715), is a particularly good example of this. During this period, and, for a period after as well, there was much more of a blend between femininity and masculinity, both in terms of public behavior and in fashion. It's very interesting to see how the social norms and the social construct of fashion in terms of gender change over time.

Why do you think people fear degendering fashion today?

Alok Vaid-Menon: I spend a lot of time thinking about this. And you know, even from a functional perspective it really makes no sense. If it were 100°F (38°C) outside in the summer, then every man would benefit from wearing a skirt instead of a suit. It's just more functional.

Gjoko Muratovski: There are many cultures where men wear sarongs, which are essentially fabrics wrapped around their waists like skirts.

Alok Vaid-Menon: Exactly. Where I'm from in India, in South India in particular, we have sarongs that are called the lungi or the dhoti. That's what men wear there because it's so hot outside. Having a wider variety of

103

things to wear, depending on the circumstances, would actually improve everyone's life, from a practical standpoint. And this is an indication that the resistance that we are experiencing today is not rational. What we are dealing with is an emotional, psychological, and traumatic resistance.

Gjoko Muratovski: How is all of this related to the idea of individuality? On paper, Western society celebrates the idea of individuality. But in practice, it fears, it mocks, or it despises individuality.

Alok Vaid-Menon: The irony is that people like me, who are visibly different, are accused of wearing a costume. But truthfully, the costume is the uniform that society gives to people so that they don't stand out. I think that we've been disciplined, especially in the Western world, into this idea that you should be part of a matrix. Standing out of this matrix means that you have chosen to put yourself in harm's way, or that somehow you think that you're better than other people. All of these connotations are then added to the idea of individuality. And what I find ironic in the United States is the whole rhetoric of freedom, when, in fact, we have a compulsory conformity here. Freedom is just rhetoric, not a daily practice. I think that people are afraid of looking different and they would rather opt to look the same, interchangeable, and homogenous.

I experience this a lot in the winter because in winter everyone starts wearing grey and black. I find this so confusing. Personally, in winter I like to wear bright-colored coats and neon heels. I feel warm, like everyone else, but people stare at me as if there is some kind of fear of color. Because of this response that I get, I've been trying to understand why there's a fear of color within the Western aesthetic sensibilities. So, I came across this really amazing book called *Chromophobia*, which is about the fear of color. In this book, the author traces how so much of the colonial encounter was about dismissing non-Western nations and Indigenous people as being brightly colored, as not matching, as vibrantly patterned, as ornamentalized, which is the word that they would use.

Then, if we look at this in a more contemporary context, much of the Western modernity and Western aesthetics was actually about resisting adornment. There was a Viennese architect named Adolf Loos who, at the beginning of the twentieth century, wrote a famous essay called *Ornament and Crime*. And in his essay, he basically makes the argument that Europe civilization and the Western civilization have evolved from ornamentality and accessorizing, and should now move to streamlined aesthetics. To pursue ornamentation in a modern society, according to him, is as bad as committing a crime.

Gjoko Muratovski: Yes, I am very familiar with the work of Alfred Loos. This particular essay, despite being utterly bizarre from a contemporary standpoint, it still represents one of the seminal modernist theories that laid the foundations of the entire modernist movement in the Western world and beyond.

Design in the Age of Change

Alok Vaid-Menon: And as a result, what we actually see is a multi-century-long project of streamlining design, and let say fashion in particular, into a uniform. I think we can only understand this in a post-Fordist capitalist mentality of mass production. Part of the way that mass fashion production works—and I am talking about brands like Gap or H&M here—is that they are basically trying to create a trope that can be reproduced over and over again.

Gjoko Muratovski: This is why I, personally, value style more than I value fashion. Fashion is a temporary construct. Style, on the other hand, has longevity. This is a form of expression that goes beyond fashion. There is also more depth to the style. I can tell more about a person that has a style, than a person that pursues fashion. Style is a reflection of the character of the individual, while fashion is a reflection of where society is at this moment. Style is what you create. Fashion is what is created for you.

Alok Vaid-Menon: I also view style and fashion in a similar way. For me, there is also a distinction between style and fashion. Fashion is what is marketed to us in a form of a template, in the sense that you buy fashion, you buy a prepackaged idea of what does it mean to be something or someone. Style, on the other hand, is about the reclamation of fashion for your own individual sartorial and aesthetic choices. What I actually am committed to is anti-fashion.

The larger spiritual crisis is that the majority of people don't know how to express themselves. We live in a template culture that requires people to fit into certain categories and boxes and they only know who they are in relation to those predetermined categories and boxes.

Gjoko Muratovski: When I was travelling around the Pacific Islands, I learned that in the Polynesian culture, there is a widely accepted notion of third gender. Have you come across that?

Alok Vaid-Menon: Yes, totally.

Gjoko Muratovski: I find this very fascinating. You may assume that in a global metropolitan area such as New York City, the notion of third gender will be far more accepted, given the diversity of people there. But no, it is not. And then, you come across small Polynesian communities who live on remote islands in the Pacific, and you find that this notion is readily embraced. Their society recognizes that individuals who do not identify as female or male are a normal part of the social fabric of the community. They even have a specific word for this.

Alok Vaid-Menon: Fa'afafine.

Gjoko Muratovski: Yes. And men in these parts also traditionally wear sarongs instead of pants.

Alok Vaid-Menon: One of the points that I really try to make when I'm speaking about degendering fashion is that if you look at Indigenous non-Western communities, they've been doing this since the very beginning.

Design in the Age of Change

I grew up with men wearing skirts, but they weren't called skirts, they were called lungis or mundus and that was not a big issue.

So much of what we imagined to be a masculine or feminine silhouette is actually a contemporary Western construct. I think the only way to really diagnose this contemporary moment is to understand nationalism and to understand how governmental regimes have a vested interest in creating populations that are conforming.

Style and fashion have always been political for me. Frankly, it baffles me when people dismiss fashion as being superficial. I think that fashion can serve as a profound space of political resistance. For example, what I wear can fundamentally shift not just the way that people treat me but also the very space that I'm in. If I walk around a street in New York City in a miniskirt, my presence fundamentally shifts that space. While we don't have that language yet to describe fashion as a force of politics, I think what I'm really trying to do, especially as an activist and as an artist, is to get people to realize that how we dress is a form of a political statement.

So often people will say, "I don't care about fashion, I just wear what I wear." That's already a political statement. There's no neutrality when it comes to style. We're all engaging in a mode of communication whenever we choose what to wear. We often forget that the majority of communication is non-verbal. It's not often about what we're saying, it's rather more about what we look like. Fashion can shift the modes of perception. With the way I dress, I shift people's very perception of what it means to be a man or what it means to be a woman. When people see me, they have to question their own gender. They need to ask themselves, "Am I as secure as I thought that I was in my manhood or my womanhood?" And then some may realize that they are not, and then these people resort to violence. When people are secure about who they really are, then they don't really have a problem with people like myself.

That's why I think that fashion is so important. And that's why I think that the work that you do right now, Gjoko, is so important. We need more academics like you to write and think critically about style and fashion. As a society, we need to engage with these deeper questions of humanity.

Gjoko Muratovski: You're absolutely right, Alok. Fashion as a concept is a much more complex idea than people realize. Both fashion and style are all about making a statement. What you wear every time you go out in public projects a statement about yourself. With your clothes and your accessories, you choose what you're saying about yourself. Even people who say, "I don't care about fashion, I'll just wear whatever," they are also making a statement. They're making a very conscious statement to project something about their beliefs by what they are wearing. As you said, you cannot be neutral in fashion. And this is what makes your activism very thought provoking in so many ways.

Based on our conversation, we can argue that the framework that our society uses today to define the notion of gender or sex is essentially a cultural construct. However, mainstream society still primarily views such things only in biological terms. What would you say are the negative effects of this for transgender and gender non-conforming people?

Alok Vaid-Menon: Yeah, you know, I always bring up one book that changed my entire life and made me give up gender. It's called *The Invention of Women* and is by Oyèrónké Oyěwùmí. She's a Nigerian feminist who traces how Western discourse of gender was imposed on Indigenous Yoruba people, in what is now Nigeria, as part of the British colonization. One of the things that she points out is, that in the West, there's this idea that your physical body correlates with your social identity. That, however, is a culturally contingent phenomenon within the Western world. She calls this a bio-cultural logic— where your visual cues signify who you are as a person.

As she points out, in the traditional Yoruba society, people were not divided by gender, but by age. The Yoruba elders had the power—regardless of their gender—which meant that any divisions of matrilineal and matriarchal traditions have been erased. This is one of the many examples that show that our world is not one dimensional. I highlight this publication to actually remind people that in the West there's this fiction that the body and biology are fixed, and that gender and culture are the things that are changing.

Every time when the mainstream society follows this idea, trans and gender-nonconforming people face dire consequences. Some people find it easier to eliminate us than to challenge this paradigm. In 2020 alone, and the year is not finished yet, there have been more than

Why do we fear gender-neutrality?

350 reported murders of trans and gender non-conforming people all across the world. That means that on average, every 32 hours a trans person is murdered. And that's a conservative estimate because we don't actually have accurate data on this. Oftentimes, when we're attacked and killed, we are misgendered by the media. What I can also say is that 2020 is the most deadly year ever for trans and gender-neutral people in the recorded history of the United States. So far, there have been over 35 murders of trans and gender non-conforming people here.

The violence against trans and gender non-conforming people inspired by this "biological determinism" has nothing to do with us. We get recruited into a worldview that is so fragile and insecure that it can't coexist with anything that calls it into question. As with any under-developed political fantasy, whenever you can't actually debate with something, you just try to destroy it—and we have seen this many times throughout history. The main-stream society wants those who question the mainstream groupthink, to disappear.

There is this constant pressure on us to disappear our-selves within the binary. We are pressured to be less visi-ble, in order to be more comfortable. But I actually don't think that we should have to change anything about what we look like. I think that others should change the way that they think about us.

What we as a trans movement are actually trying to push forward is the idea of self-authorship and self-creation. Biological determinism reduces you to a body without asking you what do you feel about yourself. Here I would also like to make a reference to Sylvester, who

111

was an amazing disco drag queen in the 1970s. When they would ask them why are they dressed in that way, they would say, "I'm just being myself." And I think that this simple statement is one of the most revolutionary frameworks that we can use to counteract this biological determinism that is being forced upon us.

Gjoko Muratovski: One of the issues that we are generally experiencing is that trans people are often objectified. Because of that, most people don't quite understand the everyday struggles that gender non-conforming people encounter in their lives. Would you be comfortable with sharing some parts of your own experiences and some of the challenges that you have encountered in your life?

Alok Vaid-Menon: You know, I grew up in a conservative small town in Texas and I thought that by living in New York City I would experience so much more acceptance. My illusion was that this city was somehow more progressive. In some ways it is, but in other ways, it is not. Every single day that I go outside, I'm afraid for my physical safety because I'm exposed to hundreds, if not thousands, of people who may want to harm me.

I don't know what these people are going through. I don't know what trauma they have. I don't know what their ideologies and their politics are. People often displace themselves on me by engaging in constant verbal and physical harassment. Sometimes people follow me home, throw trash on me, or take photos of me without my consent. Then they post these photos of me online,

112

as memes, to ridicule me. They make a spectacle out of me, and the reason why they do this is because they want to say to everyone, "If you stand out, we are going to punish you."

I know that I'm often only hearing the people who have visible negative reactions, but I'm willing to bet that there are also thousands of people who internally are thinking, "That's possible? Could I do that?" And that's why I keep doing what I'm doing. I am not doing this to get immediate reactions from people who are underdeveloped in their own healing practice, but because I want to show that it's possible to live a life outside of the Western gender binary. That it is possible to live a life on your own terms, and that living itself is an art form. For me, my poetry, my fashion ... those are all just extensions of my art. The way I live my life, the energy that I am producing in a given moment, all of that is my art.

And maybe this brings up again the Harry Styles *Vogue* cover from this morning. In some ways, people are more comfortable with visible displays of gender non-conformity if it is presented to them under the umbrella of art. For many people, it's probably okay if gender non-conformity is presented in an art gallery, or if it's featured on a magazine cover, or if it's presented on a billboard. But then the minute you see it next to you in public, it becomes a problem.

At this moment, we have masculine cis people like Harry Styles who are wearing women's clothing and that's amazing. But they get congratulated for it because they're just doing it for an editorial shoot. Whereas people like me, who are doing this every single day, outside in public with no film crew, we don't experience that sense of accolade or celebration. That is why a lot of my work is trying to get people to understand that it's not enough to just ambition to be featured on a billboard, or on a fashion runway. We have to create a society in which everyone can look like whatever they want, wherever they want.

Gjoko Muratovski: May I share an observation with you? I'm curious to hear your thoughts on this. I think that the lack of broader conversation on these topics contributes toward misgendering and contributes toward violence on people who look differently and behave differently than the mainstream society. There is no doubt that the concept of gender binary is very strongly ingrained in the mass subconscious and overcoming this is a challenge. I also notice that even cisgender people, who want to look beyond this, often don't know how to do that. In some cases, people avoid engaging with transgender individuals out of fear of offending them by accident—simply because they don't know what the social expectations of the transgender and gender nonconforming community are. My impression is that not everyone is hostile, or wants to be hostile. Some people want to be supportive or at least want to have an open mind, but they don't know how to communicate this. I'm sure that you have come across this as well, and I am wondering, what is your take on this?

Alok Vaid-Menon: Right, I totally agree with you on this. I think that there are many people that are open and receptive. They just don't know how to express that. That's why I wrote the book *Beyond the Gender Binary*. What I tried to do in this book is to list all the arguments that are used against trans and gender non-conforming people and to provide responses to them. What I wanted to do with this book is to improve gender literacy for the general public, because I think that right now, most of these gender topics are relegated to the academy and to high theory. Currently, only people who are trained academics or more specifically, people who studied the theory of post-structuralism, have access to a critique like we are having right now—on biology as a cultural phenomenon. This is a complex topic and I wanted to find a way to translate this for the masses. So, I wrote this book, which is written at a 12-year-old reading level, where I explain these things to people by using various metaphors that can help them understand this.

And also, I genuinely feel that it's okay to be wrong if it's coming from a commitment to being better. I know that lot of people are afraid of being offensive, but the way that we learn is often by messing things up. So what actually holds us back is the fear of being wrong. My advice would be to embrace vulnerability and to move forward with your best intentions, but to know that you might say things that are insensitive and to accept this as a part of your growth. I think that most trans people are actually okay with that. We'd much rather have people who are committed to learning than people who are hostile.

Gjoko Muratovski: I appreciate you sharing your thoughts on this. I find this very encouraging because

I believe that most people would like to engage in a positive way. The concern that most people have is that there seems to be this notion that nowadays people almost want to be offended, and many are using such opportunities to vilify others instead. I don't think that having such counter conversations is as productive as some people think. In fact, I find this to have quite the opposite effect. I think that what you're saying is far more progressive and more positive.

You don't need to be confrontational to get your message across. When a confrontation happens, the two parties are being distanced further away from each other. Confrontation doesn't create the setting that you need to bridge the differences and address the misconceptions. Confrontation only entrenches people further in their own beliefs.

Alok, as my final question, what would be your advice to any trans or gender non-conforming young people who are struggling to embrace their own identity. What would you say to them?

Alok Vaid-Menon: My advice is the following: I can't give you a magic potion to make things easier. All I can do is say that you have to jump into the discomfort and figure things out as you go. I think that we keep on waiting to see a road paved with rainbows, but this is just not going to happen unless we build it. All I can say is that I was in a similar place. I was terrified. I was scared of expressing myself. I have experienced a lot of pushback, but I also found so much joy on the other side. And I don't think that we speak enough about that joy. The joy of being able to look in the mirror every day and say, "I chose this form. I'm happy in this form."

And then I think the second thing I would say is really about learning trans history. This makes things feel so much more possible. It was only through learning trans history that I learned that there have always been people like me. And this is not something that I learned in school. I had to find out about these things elsewhere—in books and photographs. I was able to see photos, images, and glimpses that there are people like me. This gave me the confidence to recognize that I am part of a longer lineage or legacy and that I am a part of a community that has been responsible for many big cultural, aesthetic, and creative achievements. There have always been people like me who've been contributing to society in many positive ways. So even though you might feel new or lonely, remember that you're actually a part of this deeper historical legacy.

This is what has given me the courage and the conviction to do what I do because I know that other people like me have felt this way, and they have done the same things before me.

Gjoko Muratovski: Alok, I really appreciate you sharing your insights and personal experiences with me. I enjoyed having this conversation with you.

Alok Vaid-Menon: Thanks so much for having me, Gjoko. It's been a wonderful conversation. Thank you.

What's it like to deal with racism?

In conversation with Randall Wilson

In addition to everything else going on 2020 also exposed the deep divide that exists in the education sector in America. As the nation witnessed a resurgence of the Black Lives Matter movement, many White Americans still refuse to accept the existing inequalities in their society. In many ways, Black students don't have the same access to education as their White peers and, as a result, they are only marginally represented in the student body. The same applies to the representation of Black faculty in universities across the country. At the Ullman School of Design, we have nothing to be proud of when it comes to this matter. We only have two Black faculty in the entire school—one male (untenured) and one female (tenured). In terms of our student body, only 2.7 percent of them are Black, yet we are based in a city where close to half of the population is African American.

In the early 1980s, Randall Wilson was the only Black student studying Fashion Design at the Ullman School of Design. Then, some years later, he joined the school as an Adjunct Professor in the Fashion Design program from which he graduated. He has been teaching here for the last two decades. Randy was—and still is—the only Black male faculty member. Although he always maintained an interest in fashion design and fashion illustration, in the meantime, he also worked with numerous social service support programs. He taught special needs students at a local high school, he assisted HIV/AIDS patients with their daily tasks and distribution of their medicine, he provided assisted living services to people with mental disabilities, he served as a rehabilitation manager for criminal offenders, and he even worked as a probation officer for the Adult Parole Authority. At the start of the 2020 academic year, I have expanded the school's leadership team by appointing Randy as a Diversity and Inclusion Coordinator.

Gjoko Muratovski: Randy, over the past few years since I've been here, students from underrepresented minorities have often described you as a mentor, ally, and as a role model. This was before you were appointed to your new role as a Coordinator. What it is that you do that resonates with these students so much?

Randall Wilson: Role model is a pretty lofty description. Thank you for that, Gjoko. I'd like to see myself as an alternative to what's been fed to a lot of young creative people—especially Black, Hispanic, and Asian people, and those who may be LGBTQI+. I think that it's really important for them to have examples of achievement, progress, and tenacity. This is important because good examples can serve as blueprints for them that they can use to navigate through the complexities of life. They need to be reassured that they are in the right place and that they should hang in there, make a difference, and be the difference.

Gjoko Muratovski: I think that this is also very important for students who come from financially disadvantaged households, have underprivileged backgrounds, or those who may be first-generation students coming to university. For them, it's also very important to have somebody that can understand them, shares the same background like them, and can talk to them about the challenges and the opportunities of getting a degree in a way that resonates with them. Many of these students—and first-generation students especially—have a real need to talk to someone who can give them education-based advice or career-oriented advice that they cannot get at home.

Randall Wilson: Absolutely, and I can speak to that. I understand well what it means to come from a difficult background and the transformation that education can create for you. My first job in "fashion" as a Visual Fashion Coordinator at one major department store came after I graduated from this school. Ironically, this was the same place where years before I worked as a part of the maintenance crew, cleaning restrooms and vacuuming the dressing rooms. For most of my life, I have been using the "side door" approach to

121

access opportunities that were denied to me from the "front porch."

When I was a student, in the late 1970s and early 1980s, I often "couch-surfed" with friends because I couldn't go back home if I had to stay late at school to study. The bus would stop running at seven o'clock in the evening, and I often had to make a decision to either end what I needed to do at school, or just connect with friends and say, "Hey, can I crash at your house?" I was basically a nomad for several years while I was in school.

For me, that was "falling on the sword" but I'm glad I did it. I knew that I needed to do that because I felt that fashion was my calling. I took the opportunity to get an education in this area very seriously, and I am very grateful for that. So, what I would like to tell young people is to be on the move and sacrifice all that you can because you'll get all that back. You'll get all of that back, and then some, if you make that first sacrifice for your talent or your gift.

Gjoko Muratovski: How would you describe your experience venturing into the creative industries?

Randall Wilson: I don't think the populace here still understands what is it to be Black and be in a creative field. It's not easy. And let me be specific to Cincinnati when I say this. Cincinnati is not the sexiest city. You don't see a lot of colorful people doing colorful things around here. There are pockets and cliques of them, but you don't have a very large representation of really cool-looking, funky, unconventional people walking around.

What's it like to deal with racism?

A lot of young Black men who want to have a career in the arts or in fashion, also have to overcome prejudices in terms of the identity that society projects on certain professions. For example, when I was studying fashion, the general opinion was that "fashion equals gay." If you like fashion, you like to dress well, you like to draw clothes, then you must be gay. That was the general perception. A lot of times that's true [Laughs]—me being a case in point; but sometimes it isn't. And we still have a challenge of attracting young men to study fashion because of the societal perception that this is only a profession for gay men and women. It is not.

Gjoko Muratovski: Your personal story is a story of overcoming adversity in many ways. Would you mind sharing a little bit more about your own life journey?

Randall Wilson: I come from a different generation. I was born in 1960, and I've seen some really bad things growing up. I have been on the front line of some terrible racial biases. I have experienced some really brutal, ugly, and nasty instances. I remember being a kid and going out with my mom and my siblings to eat somewhere, and we were asked to leave many times because we were Black. I have many of these "classic" racism experiences.

I guess I was fortunate that I could take art classes in high school, commercial art in particular, which is the old term for graphic design. This is when I realized that I had a gift for arts and design. This is how from there on I went to the University of Cincinnati to study fashion design later on. And I was the only

Black design student in the early 1980s. I guess they said at the time, "Let him in, what harm can it do? He's the only one."

I was treated like an anomaly and quite frankly like something exotic; I was objectified. But while they were watching me, I was watching them. I was learning behaviors of affluent White people by observing my surroundings. I also learned how to use my physical appearance to my advantage. As I was the only one, they were curious to see what kind of work I will do, and this allowed me to showcase my talent. My talent didn't really change their minds about me, as talent doesn't change people's minds, but they learned to respect me. They respected the work that I did, and the money that they could generate from the work that I did. They were more relaxed around me, but their minds did not necessarily change. Many years later I am still here, and I am still the only one.

Gjoko Muratovski: The hiring processes within the university environment rarely depends on single individuals. Most people assume that it is the senior leadership that makes these decisions, but this is not the case in public institutions such as this one. Almost always, it is randomly selected committees that make the hiring decisions; a group of peers decide who gets hired to an academic post. Yet, nationwide, just over 5 percent of all full-time faculty members in higher education are Black—and this is with the increase in numbers that we have seen in the last decade. Why do you think that this is still the case, Randy?

What's it like to deal with racism?

Randall Wilson: A lot of change is happening today, but there is a lot of change that isn't. You can't change everything and everybody, because racism is in the DNA of America. It's in the soil, and we're digging up old bodies of discontent and disenfranchisement. We are digging up all these things now and it's ugly.

Gjoko Muratovski: How was your experience as a student back in the day?

Randall Wilson: I look back on it now and I like to think that I had a fun time as a student, but I also remember that the biases that some staff and teachers had were glaring. Some even stepped very close to the line of calling me the "N word" at times. When you're the only one, people feel like they could prod you, pick at you, and devalue you. And I'm the type of person that would not just step aside. I was born into and came through, some serious discrimination and racism. I had the grit and the resilience to overcome these challenges. I stood tall and I was living in my own truth. This sounds very corny to me now, but I was unconditionally Black, gay, and aware of my gifts and creative talents. I was very conscious about who I am. I was not going to run away from this. Where I was going to run, anyway? And for how long would I keep running before I would hit that wall again?

Gjoko Muratovski: I arrived in the United States in 2016 to take on the position of the Director of the Ullman School of Design. As an outsider at the time, I wasn't familiar with many aspects of the American culture when I arrived, and I also wasn't aware of the extent to which the society was divided here. Frankly, I was very surprised of what I came to see in terms of racial disparity. But this also meant that I didn't carry any of this inherent socio-cultural baggage with me. As a result, you and I could have very different conversations from the very beginning.

Randall Wilson: Exactly. But, it's not just the American culture that you had to learn. You also had to learn the Cincinnati culture, which is a different culture unto itself. You had a big learning curve because the American Midwest culture is very conservative. We live in a "red" state, and we have a "red" city culture here. The Midwest is heavily Republican and, on top of this, greater Cincinnati also borders with the South, which is another story altogether.

Most White people, including many of our faculty here, live in one of the three major affluent neighborhoods of Cincinnati, while most Black people live in areas that are considered to be poor neighborhoods. The White faculty don't have a relationship with the Black students, and vice versa, because they don't know how to really connect with each other. When they all go home to their neighborhoods they are surrounded by people who look just like them, think just like them, and behave just like them.

So, it took an outsider—you—to come in and shake things up. And the fact that you even took the time to talk to my students as many times as you did in my classroom is a whole new thing. You came as a stark contrast to the passive aggression that was prevalent here and in this city. You have been an agent of change, Gjoko.

What's it like to deal with racism?

Gjoko Muratovski: Thank you, Randy. I really appreciate you saying that. You know, over the past few years, I tried hard to introduce a new culture in the school, to diversify further the school's leadership team, and to create new opportunities for our Black students and for other students from underrepresented minorities. We received the first recognition of these efforts in 2017 when we were named a "Diversity Champion" by *Insight into Diversity*—the oldest magazine devoted to diversity and inclusion in higher education when compared to other design schools in the country. Following this, *Metropolis*, the leading industry publication in the field of design and architecture, called us a "game changer," and ranked us as the No. 1 design school in the United States when it comes to implementing equity and diversity initiatives—with the Harvard Graduate School of Design coming in the second place. Earlier this year, with the generous support from Procter & Gamble, we even established a half-a-million dollar scholarship fund to attract more Black students to join the school. Alongside your appointment this year, I have also appointed three Endowed Professors that are coming from underrepresented minorities—one per each of the three core disciplines in the school.

These are all good things and we are making some good progress, but we are still nowhere near where we need to be as an institution. Now, with your help, I hope that we can continue to move these things further.

I always believed in the contributions that you were making here—by representing a different voice, and for always standing up for your students, especially those who see

127

themselves as different from the others. You have always been a great advocate for diversity and inclusion, and this is the reason why you are in this role right now. Your life experience and personal journey has made you the perfect candidate for such a role.

Randall Wilson: Thank you, Gjoko. Yes, I have always done that and I will continue to do this in any way I can. And the reason why I have always been able to connect with the students in the way that I do is because I'm being authentic when I talk to them. Young people can see when someone is "real." They have a laser-sharp vision when it comes to that.

I think that too often, educators don't render themselves transparent or vulnerable to the students. This doesn't mean that they should come in and talk to them about your personal life or any of that. But they should be who they really are and they should try to actively listen to the students. I think that this makes a lot of difference. Sometimes, you don't really know who these young people are. Sometimes, they may not have been listened to their entire young lives. So to have someone who is educating them, to listen to them as well, is a major thing to them.

Gjoko Muratovski: Let's expand our conversation further and talk about cultural appropriation. This is something that frequently happens in the world of fashion. The communities that serve as a form of inspiration often perceive cultural appropriation as a disrespectful act. Black culture is one of those cultures that are often appropriated by the fashion industry. What is your take on this?

Randall Wilson: I find this act to be disrespectful because this is an industry that is appropriating our culture without investing in our talent. If they want to use our culture, or exploit our culture, they should at least invest in our culture as well. How many Black designers do these fashion labels actually have on staff? Not nearly enough in order to justify the level of appropriation that is taking place. And the same goes for other cultures that are being regularly appropriated.

Gjoko Muratovski: We live in times of great social unrest and racial divide, especially in the United States. In 2013, the Black Lives Matter movement started as a social media response against violence and systemic racism toward Black people. Today this movement has grown to become a global phenomenon. Do you see elements of that showing up in your classes?

Randall Wilson: The Black Lives Matter movement started when a young Black woman—an activist—tweeted #BlackLivesMatter. This was in response to the many incidents when the police killed unarmed Black men, women, and children.

I didn't really see any elements of this showing up in my classes when the movement emerged in 2013, but I am seeing them now, several years later.

Design in the Age of Change

I see this showing up, subtly, but in very powerful ways. For example, in my fashion illustration classes, I see Black students drawing themselves as models. That's a very strong statement. Due to the strong Euro-centric legacy of the field, we are conditioned to drawing White models. For me to see the Black self-conciseness of these young students breaking this mold is pretty amazing. And what is interesting to me is that I also see White students starting to draw people of color in their sketches, and this is because they have Black friends and friends of other races. These young people are different from the previous generations. They are more socially aware and they grew up consuming other people's culture.

But let's be fair, not all White students are embracing this new social change. They are not, and that's fine. That's their journey. One thing that I've learned to do is not being in people's faces asking them, "Why aren't you changing?" You can't force someone to change and I think that this is the disconnect that a lot of people have. Let people change when they need to change, if they want to change. This is like trying to force somebody to come out if you think that they are gay. You can't force anybody to do anything. These are all things that are very personal to people. You have to allow people to journey through that. For many people, this is a spiritual process. They need to reach their own truth. You can show them the way, but you can't force your truth down on anyone.

What's it like to deal with racism?

Gjoko Muratovski: Randy, thank you for everything you do. You are an inspiration.

Randall Wilson: And thank you for what you do as well, Gjoko. I hope that whoever comes across our conversation will digest it and will allow for these views to sink in because that's how change happens.

What's wrong with design education?

In conversation with Don Norman

Designers today are often asked to address new kinds of problems at scales quite different from those of the past, yet the way we teach design has not changed as much. The new design problems focus less on discrete artifacts for communication and manufacture and more on a diverse range of designed processes, services, complex sociotechnical systems, and communities. As the field of design continues to receive greater attention from industry, government, and society, many new opportunities are starting to emerge. However, the vast majority of university-based design programs are not equipped well to educate future designers on how to address these opportunities.

The field of design today needs to provide an in-depth, evidence-driven academic foundation for human-centered design decisions. We now need a new platform for a new form of design education—one that will help designers become advocates for social and environmental responsibility. The new generation of designers must have different preparation for a practice in a world that is much different to the one that emerged during the early industrial era. Designers today must understand the historical influences upon the world, the role of colonization (and the resulting decolonization movement), and the economic and political realities involved in any large, complex project. These are the conditions that triggered Don Norman to question how we teach design and to start a new global initiative aimed at rethinking design education for the twenty-first century.

Don is a person who doesn't need much introduction. He is the former Vice President for Advanced Technology at Apple and, for the past five years, he served as the Director of the Design Lab at the University of California San Diego (UCSD). Don is widely recognized as the ultimate authority on all matters related to user experience and human-centric design. He is best known for his books on design, especially *The Design of Everyday Things* and *Emotional Design*. The Future of Design Education initiative that Don co-founded with Karel Vredenburg from the IBM Global Design Group has been generously supported by their respective organizations, it has been sponsored by the World Design Organization, and is endorsed by a number of other high profile companies such as Procter & Gamble, J.P. Morgan, and Philips. I'm very proud to be a part of this initiative and to serve as a founding member of the steering committee.

Gjoko Muratovski: Don, let's talk about how the Future of Design Education initiative came about. I was involved

What's wrong with design education?

with this initiative from the very beginning, but it was you who started it. What inspired you to do this?

Don Norman: I am really concerned about design as a field. Design, first of all, is not well understood and this is because of its history. If you look at the history of design, it came from several different origins—art being one of these. Artists are wonderful, don't get me wrong, but it really bothers me that so many schools of design are part of art schools. There is a big difference between art and design.

Yes, like art, we too have an aesthetic side to what we do. We are both trying to give people new experiences, new thoughts, and new ways of viewing the world. But artists are expressing themselves. There is nothing wrong with that. In fact, that's wonderful—it proves humanity.

That's not what design is.

As designers, we are not designing for ourselves. We are designing for the world. We are designing for other people. With our work, we try to change society, hopefully for the better. Work like that doesn't come out of art schools.

Gjoko Muratovski: I know exactly what you mean. Half of my design education comes from very traditional European art schools and art academies.

Don Norman: Did you know that the designers that I admire most, almost every single one of them were not trained in design? Design, as a field, has a lot of problems.

Design in the Age of Change

In 1971, Victor Papanek—a very famous Industrial Designer at the time—wrote a book called *Design for the Real World*. He made the following statement: "There are professions more harmful than industrial design, but only a few." Then he said, "Well, maybe there is one field that's more harmful—advertising design, in persuading people to buy things they don't need, with money they don't have, in order to impress others who don't care." And that's true. Advertising convinces people to buy the crap that designers design.

Gjoko Muratovski: I have that book here in my library, actually. I know very well what you're talking about. That was a very interesting debate in the early 1970s. Not only Papanek but also others were very critical of design during this period, and rightfully so. Advertising, in particular, was very negatively viewed during that period. Not that its reputation is much better nowadays.

Don Norman: I think that Papanek was wrong. And here's why. The sentiment that he was voicing was absolutely correct, but what he was wrong about was claiming that everything bad was the fault of the designers—as if designers could do anything about it. The reality is that designers, because of their education, usually hold middle-level positions. In a company, if you're in the middle level, you have to do what your boss tells you—or more importantly your boss's boss—or else you're fired. As a designer, you have to do what you are told to do, or you will lose your job. Even if you run your own design studio, the same thing applies—your bosses are your clients.

What's wrong with design education?

You have to do what they tell you, or you don't get the job, and, therefore, you can't pay salaries. Designers have almost no say on key matters.

So that's one reason why design education must change.

Gjoko Muratovski: That is actually a very interesting point. And it's true, in many cases. However, nowadays we do have designers holding very senior-level positions in companies. We actually both know designers who hold such positions.

Don Norman: Yes, we do, but that is still very rare. There are very few designers like that. Designers, who hold such senior positions, hold these positions because they are more than just designers.

As you know, traditional design education is typically focused on four years of learning how to draw, and learning about materials, and learning about form and structure. And, as a result, people produce wonderful, beautiful artifacts that we love. But we need more than that.

Take a look at Apple. The world's best industrial designers there make beautiful, wonderful hardware, but they don't understand people. Apple used to be famous for that. You could just pick up your computer and use it without ever reading a manual. And today, on the iPad or the iPhone, everything is mysterious. No words—because words are ugly. Just icons, or even no icons, and you have to memorize all these ways of flipping. Do you swipe up or down, or left or right, or one finger or two fingers or three fingers? Do you tap, or tap and hold? Do you swipe up halfway and then hold your finger? Or do you have to swipe not from the very top, or from partially down and then down?

It's crazy, but when you leave such things only to designers with traditional design education, that's what they end up doing.

Gjoko Muratovski: What else do you think that we need to teach?

Don Norman: We need to teach people how to work with multidisciplinary teams.

Here is an example: Let's say that you want to cure some of the diseases that we have here in San Diego. You will need to send in healthcare workers to tend to the sick. But, the diseases are often caused by bad sanitation. So we need to fix the issue with sanitation first. And why is the sanitation bad? Well, because there aren't any restrooms or places where you can clean up if you find yourself in the middle of the city. And the people who are suffering the most from bad sanitation and these diseases are the homeless. The answer is that if you want to cure the epidemic in the city, you have to solve the homelessness problem first.

Addressing such a complex issue requires a very different kind of training than what designers normally receive in school. Regardless of this, I can argue that designers are ideally equipped to do this kind of work. That is because we don't know anything about any of these topics. That's a good thing. Therefore, when

What's wrong with design education?

we look at situations such as this, we can say, "I don't understand why we do things in this way." We ask stupid questions, and a stupid question is the most powerful question in the world. When someone says, "Well, that's how we've always done it," then you say, "Okay, why have you always done it that way?" And pretty soon you will discover that maybe you didn't have to do things in that way. And that's a whole new approach. All sorts of other disciplines try to solve these problems, but they look at efficiency, performance metrics, cost, and productivity. We, as designers, look at the people. The real needs of the people.

Gjoko Muratovski: That's absolutely correct, Don. We bring a human-centered focus to everything we do. This is what makes design so relevant and so sought after in areas that were previously dominated by other disciplines that would address issues from the perspective of technology, material properties, sales, commerce, or economy. The people, themselves, were never at the center; and we have brought that human perspective into the mix. Now, this all somehow seems like a very obvious thing to do, but this was rarely the case in the past.

By the way, did you know that the multidisciplinary aspect and the approach that you just described already exists in the domain of crisis leadership? There is a parallel between design thinking of this order and crisis leadership that has not been explored before. I realized this when I undertook training in crisis leadership at the Harvard Kennedy School of Government. At the time, I was pursuing a completely unrelated thing, which had

seemingly nothing to do with design. I was studying
how to deal with a crisis on a large scale. And once we
started going through principles of crisis leadership,
I could see all of the things that you just said, laying out
perfectly.

At the time we were looking at various scenarios
of crisis leadership—from a terrorist attack to a major
natural disaster. Here is one example: Let's say a major
catastrophe has happened and the entire city is on fire.
Everything is burning. In this situation, you might
assume that the fire department would know what to do
and that they can mitigate the situation. Because that's
what they do when there is a fire, right? But they can't.
This is because they are neither equipped nor trained, to
deal with a crisis on such a level.

We often assume that every response that the firefighters take is dealing with a crisis, or that every
call that an ambulance takes is dealing with a crisis.
No, for them this is a routine emergency; it's not a
crisis. For a random person, however, any emergency
scenario might be perceived as a crisis, but for these
first responders, this is just a routine. However, when
the scale and the context of the emergency changes,
then the situation becomes a crisis for them as well.
And they're not really prepared to handle the situation.
This is the moment when you need to look at things in
a completely different way.

In such a scenario, where the whole city might be burning down, you need more than firefighters to save the city.
You will need a city planner, architects, logistics experts,
the police, the hospitals, the water, and the sanitation

What's wrong with design education?

department. You will need to bring everyone on board
who has any idea of what makes a city function, to come
together and figure out a way forward. Because even people
who deal with emergencies every day—they can't address
this, because this is not an emergency under normal circumstances. Complex problems are made of multiple moving
parts, and no one can see all the pieces at once from where
they are standing. This is because each one of these subject
matter experts carries with them an implicit bias that affects
their thinking and their actions. Overcoming this implicit
bias is key to looking at the bigger picture and finding new
solutions. And this is when I realized that human-centric
designers are perfectly suited for crisis leadership because
we do not have ownership of any of these moving parts,
meaning that we do not have the implicit bias that these
other discipline-specific experts might have.

Don Norman: Why did you say that your training had
nothing to do with design? This is exactly the sort of
thing that designers are good at and should be doing.
I think that it's a failure of design that we are not doing
this already.

Gjoko Muratovski: Absolutely. The problem is that we
were never educated to think of ourselves in that way.

Don Norman: Yes, which is, again, part of the problem
when we talk about design education.

Gjoko Muratovski: Designers are really great at making
these lateral connections, facilitating such dialogues, and

as you say—asking stupid questions. Because it is like that sometimes; it does take a stupid question to provoke a smart conversation. [Laughs] But how do we teach that?

Don Norman: Well, we can teach that by asking people to work on such issues. Almost every city in the world has crises and problems that need to be dealt with. The problem is that design educators are often unaware of these issues because they're isolated. But actually, students can go out and work with people outside the university, so there is no excuse here, really. And cities need us because a lot of the other disciplines don't understand how to focus on people.

Let me give an example of today's crisis, the COVID-19 pandemic. The problem is the public health officials say that what we have to do is to isolate people for at least two weeks so that we know that they're free of the disease. And we have to be very careful not to be in a close distance with other people, and we have to also wear masks. And they have to be the right masks, etc. And this has been going on well for me. I'm in my home now, and I've been in my home basically since March. So that's, what, seven months now?

The problem is that the people who are addressing the medical issues don't really understand the economic implications of their recommendations. And they don't understand the behavioral implications either. This helped to quell the pandemic in some parts of the world, but people wanted to go back and start enjoying life again, and that invoked the pandemic to resume. Because, even though there was still a lot of disease around, people wanted to eat out, see their friends, dance, drink, whatever. The thing is that we needed more people who understood the economic impact and the behavioral impact of the lockdown from the beginning. Today, we're beginning to realize that locking everybody down is the wrong approach because not every-body is highly susceptible to the disease, and doing this could destroy our economy. And that will cause another kind of problem that we will have to deal with, as well.

So, yes, if you want to be a designer today, you need to know enough about the economy, and about human behavior, and about disease, and about managing people, and about working with very many different disciplines. That's why our education needs to change.

Gjoko Muratovski: Bruce Mau and I were discussing this recently. We both felt that designers have been a part of the problem for so long, mainly due to the lack of proper education. Designers were rarely aspiring to do anything more than what they were expected to do, which was to create face value.

Today, things are very different. Many of our gradu-ates, for example, try to change the companies where they work from within. They push and advocate for sus-tainability. They push and advocate for racial equality. They are relentless. They are not always in leadership roles, but they try from the position where they are to change things.

Don Norman: I think that doesn't work, and I'll tell you why it doesn't work. Here's why your people who say that

143

we must have sustainable products are not making them. The story that I tell, it's a slightly different story, but it's the same story nevertheless. And it goes along the lines of what we discussed at the start of our conversation.

Designers come to me and say, "My company doesn't understand me." I then say, "Okay, so how do you talk to your bosses?" and "Who is your customer?" And they tell me that their customer is the person in the store who buys the product or the person who uses their service, etc. And I say, "No. Your customer is the person who pays you. Your customer is the person you work for. Not your boss, 'cause your boss probably understands you. It's the boss of your boss. How do you talk to them?" And they say, "Oh, yeah, we talk to the highest level of the administration. We tell them what wonderful work we do and how our customers love it, and the difficulties the customers would have otherwise, and we show them the design prizes we won." And I say,

I used to be a Vice President at a very large company— Apple. And if somebody would come to me and told me that about their work, I would have said, "Yes, thank you very much. We know you're very good; that's why we hired you. And now if you'll excuse me, I have to go back to my work."

If you want to be human-centered design, then you better start understanding the people who you are working for. And they are impressed not by your prizes, but by the increased sales, decreased costs, and increased margins. And if you have a new idea that you want to share with them, then yes, you can draw some pictures or show them prototypes. But what you really need to do is to show them a spreadsheet of how your idea will increase their sales and profits.

See, one of the problems we also face is the way that our current economy works. The financial models that we use are too short-term oriented. Also, there's this widely accepted myth that a company is only responsible to its shareholders because technically, the shareholders own the company. So the company has no responsibility to their employees, neither to the customers nor to the community in which the company lives. And that's wrong, and I think it's evil. What this leads to, is focus on short-term revenues. Every quarter, every three months, the CEOs are judged on how profitable they've been. And we need to have more than this. We need to. We have to change the way we promote and reward business executives. So, for designers to succeed, we have to change how we treat our business executives because we want them to be rewarded for long-term benefits to both the company and society.

Gjoko Muratovski: I always say to our designers that one thing doesn't necessarily exclude the other. You could still do good things for the world, and be profitable. The reality is that you're not going to change the world by sitting on the sidelines.

And things are changing, Don. Many topics like global warming, climate change, social innovation, and sustainability used to sit on the margins. For many years, these topics were only a small voice out there on the outskirts of society. Today, they are mainstream topics, but they are still marginalized. So what we need to do is to flip the script. The topics are not the problem; it's how we tell their story. And if you can tell this story in a way that resonates with the decision makers, then you have a winning formula.

Don Norman: Yes. And we have to change the way people think about design. This is important because design is a way of thinking—for solving the world's most important problems. Since we are both working on this, we both know that we have a very long project ahead of us.

Gjoko Muratovski: We can see that design education is already changing in some fundamental ways as a result of all the issues that we're facing today. What have you observed so far as being the most interesting initial change that has taken place?

Don Norman: In many ways, it's the understanding that we actually have something to contribute.

Gjoko Muratovski: I think that we need to look at this on a more granular level. Yes, we do have something to contribute. The question is how we could make this contribution in a meaningful way. Most of the time, designers think that they are helping when they are not.

Don Norman: Yes, that's what designers do. We're called to solve the problem of water supply in Africa, let's say. We go in for a month or two months and do our design research, and we say, "Oh, we understand your problem." And then we do our ideation, and our testing, and our prototypes, and we come back and say, "Here's a solution to your problem." And then we wonder why our solution is not accepted. It's because, first of all, we can't tell people what their problem is and then tell people what their solution is. This is something that has to come from them. So we have to change how we design, even on this level. At the UCSD Design Lab, which is the institution that I founded, we call this a "community-driven design." We go into a community, we find the people who are already trying to solve the problem, and we help them, we tutor them, mentor them, and we facilitate what they're doing. We don't tell them what to do because they understand their problems well. They just don't have the design research skills to understand exactly what the contributing factors are.

Gjoko Muratovski: I have actually seen this particular problem, which you just pointed out, in Australia. For decades, architects, with government support, were try-ing to build housing to help the Aboriginal communities who live in the Australian Outback.

So, this Anglo-Australian government and their architects are looking at these Indigenous communi-ties, the Aboriginal people, who have lived there for the last 50,000 years, and they say, "Well, we need to help them to live better." And they go and they build them these typical Australian houses that you may see in any typical suburb in Australia, and they plant them right in the middle of the Outback, which is a very harsh

147

environment with a very unique eco-system. And then they come back a year later and they see these houses damaged, destroyed, neglected. And then they say, "There you go! These people are uncivilized. We tried our best to help them, but all of this is their fault. They don't know how to live in these nice houses." I was stunned when I saw this. This whole approach is not only ridiculous but it also shows complete disregard and disrespect to the Indigenous way of life.

The Aboriginal people who traditionally lived in the Outback were nomads. They didn't live in houses. They wandered from place-to-place as they searched for food and water. They knew how to live in harmony with the environment that was surrounding them. That was their way of life and they've been living in this way long before the British colonizers came there. Their way of life, although significantly altered, has not been completely wiped out by the colonizers. They still have their own ways for how to live with the land. They still have their own ways for cooking their food. They still have their own distinct culture. None of the traditional things that they do, that are part of their lives, fit within the design constructs that cater to the practical, functional or aesthetic needs of the Anglo-Australians. But they simply place them there, and then they wonder why they can't function in these houses. The reason why these houses are damaged is because they're trying really hard to make these houses their homes. So, they try to remove the oven because they cook differently. They try to alter certain things in these houses because they live differently. But from an Anglo perspective, this is seen as a failure of the Indigenous community to embrace a more "civilized" way of life.

This is something that is common to any colonial or postcolonial society, and is a typical problem virtually everywhere where a more dominant group is in the position to make decisions on behalf of another less dominant group. In line with this, I'll also tell you another interesting story that follows the same plotline. It's a very different story, but the lessons are the same. It's about my home city of Skopje, the capital of Macedonia.

In 1963, an earthquake destroyed 80 percent of the city. At the time, Macedonia was a part of Yugoslavia. What followed next became an incredible experiment in architecture and urban planning, of global proportions. With support from the UN and UNESCO, the whole city was reconstructed with the help of, I believe, 77 participating countries. At the time, two options were considered: to reconstruct the city as it was, or to design an entirely new city instead. The latter option prevailed. The new city was envisioned as a statement of what can happen when the world comes together. This was the first time during the Cold War that the West and the East joined forces on a common project. The idea was to take this disaster of unspeakable proportions and transform it into a vision of hope and a new beginning. I was not born yet when the earthquake happened, but years later I learned that my uncle was the mayor of the city when all of these reconstruction efforts took place.

Under the banner of the UN and UNESCO, a global team of experts was assembled. The new Master Plan for Skopje was developed by the famed Japanese architect,

149

Design in the Age of Change

Kenzō Tange. He created the new plan for Skopje by following the principles that he used to develop the Master Plan for Tokyo a few years prior to this. As one of the leading figures of the avant-garde Japanese Metabolism movement, Tange designed Skopje to feature remarkable examples of Brutalist architecture, alongside new visions and new urban concepts for city living. The new Skopje was an incredible undertaking by any standard. The idea behind all of this was so powerful that even artists like Pablo Picasso and Alexander Calder wanted to support the city by donating some of their artworks to the newly built Museum of Contemporary Art in Skopje.

I was born just as this project was coming to its end and I had an opportunity to grow up in this—what was for me at the time—a magical new city. And I have to say; growing up in this city is what inspired me to learn more about architecture, design, and art. For me, this city was great. But it was great because I didn't know how the city looked before. Growing up in this brand new city was all I knew, and I loved it. However, not everyone enjoyed living in this city.

When they were building these buildings, the architects and the urban planners had not taken into account how certain communities used to live in different parts of that city. They decided to clear out whatever was left from these neighborhoods and they put all these people into high-rise concrete blocks and designer suburbs. What these experts could not imagine at the time was that these people would not like to live like that. Skopje was a city that existed for more than millennia and people had their own inherent way of life there. Regardless of how great this utopian idea was, how visionary the architects and the urban planners were, and how good their intentions were, at the end of the day, they were in disconnect with the communities for which they were designing. In the end, the project failed. It took 50 years for this to happen, but the utopian city, as it was imagined, did not survive.

Don Norman: Both of these are great stories.

One of my favorite books is called *The Tyranny of Experts: Economists, Dictators, and the Forgotten Rights of the Poor*. It's written by William Easterly, who is an economist himself. And what he's saying is that whenever we have a major problem, we call in the world experts. We assume that because these people are experts, they best understand what the issues that we are dealing with are. The problem is, that an expert is someone who has an abstract level of knowledge and understanding. The abstraction is important. That's how you can take your expertise and understand the issues and what the problems are. But as an expert, you don't necessarily understand the people, the community, how they live, their abilities, the things they dislike, and so on. They can spend hundreds of billions of dollars and decades of work, but without truly understanding people, all of that will be wasted. And that's why I want to train designers to understand people. A community-driven design is all about co-design; it's about enabling communities to come up with their own solutions to their own problems.

Gjoko Muratovski: I think that co-design, as a concept, is probably the best thing that has happened to design in a long time. This is a process in which designers create solutions together with the people for whom they're actually designing for, by engaging the community and by taking their feedback on board. This process takes that whole arrogance out of the field of design that was present for so long. But let's be fair; designers are not the only ones who have this problem. Architects are probably worse.

Don Norman: Architects are rewarded—they're given prizes—on the basis of a photograph of their building taken from a position where nobody would ever be. Architecture is primarily focused on the exterior appearance, without much regard on how the inside works.

Gjoko Muratovski: Well, for a long-time design was awarded in the same way. The user was completely removed from the equation. Awards were given on the basis of how the design looks, not on the basis of whether it is actually useful.

Don Norman: That's why I really dislike museum exhibits of design. Take MoMA, the Museum of Modern Art in New York, for example. I've argued a lot with the design curator there. I think she agrees with me, in principle, but the problem with her exhibits is that they are only focused on artifacts. And that's not what all design is. I understand that it's hard to exhibit the thought process that went into deciding what direction the design should go. These are all very complex stories to tell. So, museums just show artifacts instead. MoMA shows beautiful coffee pots and stuff like that.

What's wrong with design education?

Gjoko Muratovski: I understand what you mean. There are things that I like about museums and galleries, and things that I don't like. And you are right. I also think that MoMA doesn't do a particularly great job of curating and displaying design well. The Cooper Hewitt Smithsonian Design Museum, on the other hand, actually did a really good job a few years ago on the power of facilitating social change by design.

Don Norman: That's one of the few large museums in the world solely devoted to design. They can spend a lot of time trying to explain what were the thought processes behind the design. In fact, what I'd love to see in a museum, and only a few museums do this, I want to see all the failed design attempts. Here is what we started with, and here is why it didn't work. That's how you learn. Designers don't like to talk about their failures, but it's the failures that are the best teaching vehicle.

Gjoko Muratovski: Procter & Gamble actually have that. They have their own Museum of Innovation where they showcase things like this. The museum is really beautiful. It's inside their corporate headquarters, here in Cincinnati. They display the products that they have created and the process that went behind that. As of recently, they started developing another section in the museum, which is about their failures; the products that failed. The executives often go on tours at the museum and they try to understand what went well, what was the context of the time, and why it went well; or what failed and why it failed. The museum has proper curators and researchers who study the history of innovation in the company. And this company, which is the largest consumer goods company in the world, is nearly 200 years old. That makes this whole thing quite amazing.

Don Norman: Now, here's what I want us to do. Next time I visit you in Cincinnati, we should do that museum.

Gjoko Muratovski: Absolutely. This museum is not open to the public, but we are all friends here. I'd be happy to arrange a tour for us next time you come for a visit.

On another note, I also wanted to ask you something. You and Karel Vredenburg from IBM Design have made a very significant effort to ensure that different voices are heard and represented in the Future of Design initiative. Let's talk more about the importance of this. Why this matters?

Don Norman: One thing that I have spent a lot of time learning about is "institutional racism." There is a wonderful book called *Monoculture* that explains this problem. Everybody knows that diversity is a good thing because it fuels innovation by bringing different points of view. We often assume that in order for us to have diversity we should just hire people from different backgrounds and different parts of the world. This, however, is the wrong approach. Leaders in various areas from around the world think in very much the same way, regardless from where they are coming from. People who are globally successful will always pass our tests when we try to hire them, and that is because we are looking for people who think just like us, even if they don't look like us.

I like to say that I am not a racist because I treat everybody the same. And when I evaluate people for employment, I also treat them all the same. I look for quality and I try to hire the best people for the job. I don't care what their gender is, I don't care what their race is, I don't care what their culture is. I want to hire people who are really good. Well, that means that I want to hire people who think just like me, and I often do this without realizing it. This is what makes me a racist and this is called institutional racism. And it's not just me who thinks in this way. I am a part of a much bigger institution, a country, and for that matter, a world that has adopted the same Western mode of thought and Western belief system. I am a part of this monoculture that makes me a racist without knowing it. And that has to change. That means changing not just me personally, but changing how we do things in the university sector as well.

Gjoko Muratovski: So, what do you think is the best way forward for us to envision the future of design education? Should we build bridges between divergent design communities? Do we need to create parallel educational systems? Or should we integrate new ways of thinking within the existing system?

Don Norman: When I start working on something new, I have no clue what needs to be done. I work hard on things I don't understand. I don't understand how everything needs to come together, how it fits together.

Usually, it takes me a few years to piece everything together and make things coherent. Right now, I'm in the incoherent stage, so I can't answer this. But the issues that you just listed are absolutely the right questions.

I don't think, however, that the final answer can come from people like you and me. I think that the answer has to come from the very people that we want to engage and from the communities that are normally left out of the conversation. All of us who are part of this initiative want for underrepresented communities to be a major part of this conversation, and that's what we will be doing in the next phase of our education program.

As designers, we need to test our ideas, try different approaches, and build new concepts. In this process, we need to observe what is working and what is not working right, so that we can modify our approach. I expect that whatever we put together won't quite be it, but our mistakes will help us move forward. Being wrong is good because being wrong is how you learn. The most important principle that always guides me is that I don't know the answer.

Gjoko Muratovski: One thing is for sure, Don. People like you and me, and others like us, will not be the ones who will define the future of design education. We have too much implicit bias in order to do that. We have spent a large part of our lives figuring out how this system works and we know how to develop effective solutions for this system. And now, when the system needs to change, it's really not up to us to work all of these things out. Whichever way you look at it, people like you and me are still in some ways a part of the problem. We are too involved with the system as is. The positive thing is that we are very conscious of that, and we have chosen to be a part of the solution. We can help, though, by paving the road for the next generation. We can help by creating a new educational platform for others to use and build upon, and we can empower new voices to start new conversations. We have a lot of tools at our disposal to enable these things to happen.

Don, thank you for starting this initative, and thank you for this conversation.

Don Norman: Gjoko, it's always a pleasure talking to you.

How can we create resilient economies?

In conversation with Ida Telalbasic

In 2020, the COVID-19 pandemic has significantly widened the global wealth inequality. At the same time, while we are witnessing rising unemployment, debt, and extreme poverty, the world's richest billionaires saw their wealth increasing by 27 percent. And even beyond this, the pandemic is now increasing the economic inequality between the wealthy countries that can afford to bail out their firms, and the poorer countries that do not have the capacity to do so. This is our "new normal" today. But does it need to be like this?

What kind of tools do we have at our disposal to create more resilient economies during a state of crisis? What kind of conditions do local communities need to create in order to thrive, while the global economy falters? Is money the only resource that we need to have access to in order to conduct our businesses or to acquire goods? Despite the general notion that we somehow exist in a fixed state of economic activity, there are many things that we can do to change the way things are. And now is the best time for us to rethink and reset how our economic system functions.

This is the topic of my conversation with Ida Telalbasic—a service design strategist with expert knowledge in alternative economies, complementary currencies, and entrepreneurial ecosystems. Ida also brings a unique global perspective to her work. She was born in Bosnia, grew up in Zimbabwe, studied in Italy, and now lives and works in the United Kingdom. Currently, she is teaching at Loughborough University London, Imperial College London, Central Saint Martins, and the University of Oxford.

Gjoko Muratovski: For a designer, your research is quite unique. You study alternative economies, which is a topic that I find quite fascinating. Can you please tell me more about your work?

Ida Telalbasic: Sure. My initial research and design started around the thinking of, "What can we do to tackle the socio-economic crisis of 2008?" That was the last major crisis we had, prior to this one now. The lessons that we learned from this crisis are relevant to the current socio-economic crisis caused by the COVID-19 pandemic.

At the time, I was doing my doctorial studies in Italy, at the Polytechnic University of Milan. My thesis was focused on service design innovation and strategic design. Soon after the 2008 crisis, I noticed that there were a lot of start-ups that were struggling to access financial services and struggling to keep afloat. I have seen early-stage entrepreneurs struggling to keep their businesses running because they didn't have enough financial capital.

As designers, we are constantly preaching how design has the capacity to bring about positive change. So, I started to ask myself, "Why are we not applying design thinking to our economic systems?" We design to influence policy, we design for healthcare, and we design for almost everything else. Why not explore design for our economies? So my questioning started around the idea of what service design can do about the current inequality of income distribution.

Gjoko Muratovski: That's really interesting. Let's unpack this a little bit more. How would you define an alternative economy?

Ida Telalbasic: Well, first I wanted to understand better what constitutes a crisis. This is how I came across the meaning of the term "crisis," which in Mandarin stands for both "danger and change." So, I decided to pursue this notion of "change" further. Does this mean that crisis as "change" can also mean an opportunity for innovation?

Coming from a design research background, I also understood that I couldn't stay purely within the service design field. I had to cut across disciplines to understand this topic better. So, I started looking at debt and credit systems and, of course, being trained as a designer, I found these economic areas quite complex and challenging. Nevertheless, I dived deeper into understanding how credit systems and alternative ways of exchange work.

What helped me in this process was the application of systems thinking. This helped me to understand better what the knowledge economy is all about. Currently, this is the economy in which we live now. And we are also living in a service economy and a digital economy. In line with this, I also started looking into behavioral economics and complementary currencies, as I found these to be important areas to consider in the context of my studies. This led me to the question, "What is the role of design in co-designing a new currency system?"

If we are struggling to secure financial capital, can we design—or actually co-create—a new currency to meet the needs of social entrepreneurs? In this process, I basically looked at creating collaborative services. When you design services that include final users in the process, then they become both the service co-designers and co-producers. This adds to the social value that these services create.

Gjoko Muratovski: When we discuss these things, we are essentially talking about creating financial resilience. Financial resilience is even more important during a state of crisis, and currently, we're experiencing at least three different crises at the same time. We have a health crisis, a social crisis, and an economic crisis. What is the key economic element that

How can we create resilient economies?

we need to consider in order to build such resilience?

Ida Telalbasic: When I was studying this issue, one of the things that I came across was the idea of complementary currency systems. We use complementary currencies all the time—vouchers, coupons, time credits, and frequent flyer points—these are all different kinds of models that we're quite familiar with. But there are also other kinds of complementary currency systems, which are capable of making a more significant economic impact. The more advanced systems can play a major role in developing the financial resilience.

One of these systems is Sardex—a very successful, business-to-business (B2B) mutual credit system that was introduced in Sardinia, Italy. This system helped local businesses to stay afloat during the 2008 crisis. When the banks stopped lending money, the local businesses were forced to create their own money in order to survive. They created their own micro-economy based on the resources that they had on the island, separate from the global economy that crashed.

And I would like to mention the Swiss WIR Bank, which offers one of the most successful, complementary currencies in the world. This bank was founded in 1934, right after the Great Depression, and between the two World Wars. What this bank did was to try and inject additional capital in the form of a mutual credit, in order to keep money circulating within the economy through continued exchange of goods and services. Their currency proved remarkably resilient during periods of economic downturn, and it runs without relying on the Swiss franc. When there's an economic crisis and the Swiss franc decreases from circulation, the WIR currency increases in circulation. When the economy is booming, the Swiss franc increases again.

In the cases of Italy and Switzerland, we have evidence that having these two complementary currencies in parallel to the formal currencies can really help keep local businesses afloat.

Gjoko Muratovski: How would you define what a complementary currency is?

Ida Telalbasic: When it comes to defining what a complementary currency really is, I like to look at the definition by Bernard Lietaer. Among other things, he was responsible for co-designing and implementing the single European currency system—the Euro. For him, complementary currencies are basically an agreement to use something else than a tender. They serve as a medium of exchange with a purpose of linking unmet needs with otherwise unused resources. And that's really interesting because here we are looking at the concept of idle capacity.

Gjoko Muratovski: What would you say are the fundamental principles behind this?

How can we create resilient economies?

Ida Telalbasic: We are living in a knowledge economy.
In a knowledge economy, not everyone has the capital
to exchange services in order to develop a business, but
we all have knowledge. So the question is, "How can we
capitalize this knowledge in a certain circuit with certain governing rules?" One thing that I think is really
interesting to mention here is that this type of thinking
is inspired by systemic biomimicry—economic systems
imitating natural systems.

Let's say, as an example, there is a panda that eats only
one type of food. The resilience of this panda will be very
low because it relies on only one type of food. If something
happens, and for some reason that food source disappears,
then the panda will starve. The human body is another
example of this form of natural resilience. We have two kidneys. If one kidney fails, we can still survive with the other
one. This is nature's way of creating resilience by providing
parallel systems for living. By following the same principle,
complementary currencies provide businesses with parallel
capital or resources.

This is one way in which if we can translate systemic biomimicry thinking into the monetary system;
diversity ensures more resilience. An important thing
is to note that complementary currencies don't aim
to substitute or replace current monetary systems,
but we very much need them. They do serve as a legal
agreement in which people believe and trust. However,
I have to note that these types of systems work differently in different regions of the world. The rules that
govern these systems differ in different contexts. The
motivations and interests in initiating these kinds of

systems also differ, as well as the benefits that they bring.

Gjoko Muratovski: I find complementary currency systems quite fascinating as a topic. Two of these systems that I'm particularly impressed by, are the microfinancing model developed by the Grameen Bank in Bangladesh, and the Torekes social currency that was introduced in Belgium. Can you, perhaps, talk a little bit more about these two models?

Ida Telalbasic: Sure. The Grameen Bank is a famous example, and it comes from Bangladesh. It was founded by the social entrepreneur, Muhammad Yunus. He won a Nobel Peace Prize for developing this microcredit system. I actually had the honor of meeting him at his book launch in London. I was really glad that I had the chance to tell him in person how he inspired my work in so many different ways.

His idea was basically to provide access to banking services to the poor from the developing world, i.e., people who don't have access to any kind of financial services like this. He wanted to find a way to provide credit to the poor, who are usually completely excluded financially in this sense. And what he developed was a system of providing microloans at favorable conditions to small groups of people, primarily women. In this system, each borrower belongs to a small solidarity group and he or she is responsible for repaying their own loan. The members are not responsible for paying each other's loans. But, if someone defaults in that system, then the

166

entire group doesn't get any more loans. So, this creates a certain kind of social pressure, where members of each group will often help each other toward reaching their repayment goals. This practice has been termed as "solidarity lending." And what is interesting, is that the members of a small group actually act as co-guarantees of repayment.

The Torekes, on the other hand, is another excellent example that comes from Belgium. There is also an interesting difference between the examples—one comes from a highly developed European country and the other one comes from a South Asian developing country. Another interesting thing is that the Grameen was founded by a private individual, whereas Torekes was established by a government.

One other thing that I should stress here is that many governments see complementary currencies as a threat to their national currencies. This is what makes the Torekes such an interesting exemption. The Belgian government was keen to support and create this currency in order to help a very poor neighborhood in the city of Ghent.

This city had a large and impoverished immigrant population, often living in very small apartment blocks. Most of these people's dream was to have some kind of land to do some gardening so that they can grow their own food. The Torekes system was developed in such a way that it enabled these immigrants to earn Torekes by conducting public goods work. For example, they could plant window boxes, collect litter, keep their neighborhood clean, and so on. Essentially, they could earn this currency by doing community work and things that would lead toward the betterment of their neighborhood. Next, the government started renting out small plots of land to these people to basically do gardening and use them for growing food. And these small rents could be paid in Torekes. People could also use Torekes in specialized supermarkets; they could buy cinema tickets at discounted rates, or buy bus tickets.

What makes this thing interesting is that the government tripled the value of the money that they initially invested in this project, in terms of benefit or what was done in return. The neighborhood was clean, they had flowers everywhere, and the communities were growing their own food. The system allowed this really interesting circulation of benefits to be focusing on making that part of the city better. This is a great example where a complementary currency can bring about behavioral change through reward.

Gjoko Muratovski: I really like how they've managed to transform that community by creating a micro-economy within the community. Furthermore, they also used the same system and currency to even create some new job opportunities. For example, they opened a Torekes Cafe, where the local people would work, selling locally made products, and cooking food made from locally grown produce. And everything, of course, could be paid for in Torekes currency. It's fascinating how such a small thing can lead to such a significant social change.

168

How can we create resilient economies?

The Grameen Bank in Bangladesh is another amazing example. And yes, in that part of the world there is a real need for the socially and economically disadvantaged communities to gain access to funds. Unfortunately, sometimes these communities are further abused by false promises of access to such funds.

One example of that is what Subrata Roy did in India with his company, Sahara India Pariwar. He created a micro-savings model for the poorest communities in India. Unfortunately, the entire model proved to be an elaborate "Ponzi" scheme where the poorest people of India lost even the tiniest savings that they had. In the process, Subrata Roy accumulated a vast fortune for himself.

Ida Telalbasic: There is always the possibility that the system can be abused if it is unregulated. Trust plays a huge part in all of this. Without trust, people can start abusing and misusing the system in many different ways.

In my research, I would always stumble upon this question of, "How much do you want to scale these types of models?" They do have their limits. I think that the danger is that if these systems or service models grow too big, then the trust could be lost. If you take Grameen as an example, we know that this model relies on the close ties between the people in these small groups and on the social pressure that they exert, thus, making sure that the members of these groups do repay their loans.

Design in the Age of Change

Gjoko Muratovski: What is interesting is the power of these systems to challenge the way money is both managed and produced by states and banks.

Ida Telalbasic: And this is where trust comes into the picture once again. One of the reasons that these systems come to exist is because people don't have trust in the local authorities or in the financial system itself. People start these localized circuits or networks in order to provide individual empowerment or to enhance collaboration between members of a community. The basic premise is to create an eco-system where communities can help each other by using their existing local resources. This is all about capacity building and building stronger community ties. There is a collaborative mindset here that helps people to realize that if they are a part of a network, they can benefit from the number of people who are in that network.

Gjoko Muratovski: What are your thoughts on Bitcoin?

Ida Telalbasic: Of course, we can't talk about this topic and not mention Bitcoin.

Bitcoin is an example of a decentralized currency system, and this is where the threat of not being able to control these kinds of systems comes into play. You also opened up the conversation of system abuse. Well, Bitcoin is one of those examples that come to my mind where misuse is definitely prevailing. Personally, I am not a huge fan of Bitcoin. This system encourages people to use huge amounts of electric energy to mine coins through mathematical algorithms. This is not positively contributing to our society, and neither is it improving our ecologies or environment in any way.

Gjoko Muratovski: What would you say are the main challenges in establishing systems like this?

Ida Telalbasic: When we talk about complementary currencies, we also need to address the question of convertibility—are people allowed to convert a complementary currency into a fiat period currency? Do we want people to enter this system, access the services and the benefits of this system, and then exit? This is a real risk because convertibility opens up the possibility of misuse. This is a real risk, which is why you need to ask yourself many questions in this process.

How would this currency work? How would you enter? How would you build your reputation? What would the exit strategy be? What would the different valuation schemes be? How would you actually be able to convert—or not convert—time, credits, or money in order for early-stage entrepreneurs to benefit in developing their services?

Service design can play a major role in overcoming some of the challenges in establishing such systems. We can't design experiences, but we can design the condition for certain experiences to take place. We can basically create ways in which we can design

interactions between people, between people and technology, and between people and business models, and
then larger communities and systems within larger
ecosystems.

Gjoko Muratovski: Ida, to round up our conversation—
what would be your advice?

Ida Telalbasic: I do want to stress that we do need more
of these types of systems. The current crisis that we are
facing due to the pandemic, and the financial crisis that
we faced in 2008, are not new or rare phenomena. There
have been many economic crises and financial crashes,
bank crashes, and sovereign debt defaults throughout
history. This is not something that happens every twenty
years or so. These things actually happen quite, quite
often.

   In addition to communities, I also think that
many companies need to start developing their own
resilience strategies from within. The more organizations are prepared for economic disruption, uncertainty, or something similar happening in the future,
the better we will all be. This is how we deal with the
shock that basically determines whether we survive
or not.

Gjoko Muratovski: I do think that the time is certainly
ripe for the introduction of new financial models. We
need to find more ways on how we can change the world
in a more positive way. And there's no better time than
during a crisis to actually do that. Thank you for sharing

How can we create resilient economies?

such fascinating insights with me, Ida. I really enjoyed having this conversation.

Ida Telalbasic: Always a pleasure talking with you, Gjoko.

How do we find comfort in unsettling times?
In conversation with Mark Boudreaux

Toys are more than just presents for children. We often take toys for granted, but they are an important part of our lives. Playing with toys helps children develop motor and cognitive skills, learn how to be creative, solve problems, and overcome obstacles. Toys also help us to learn to walk, talk, socialize, acquire knowledge, grow emotionally, and develop social and spatial awareness. However, some toys go far beyond this childhood stage of our lives and make a lasting impact, taking us into the world of nostalgia. As such, they serve as familiar cultural markers when we are confronted by change. And sometimes, when toys are connected with an additional signifier—a film, a TV series, or a cartoon that we used to watch as children—they also provide us with a sense of comfort.

Just a few months before the pandemic started, Disney+ (the video-on-demand platform of The Walt

Disney Company) launched *The Mandalorian*—a spinoff of the popular *Star Wars* film franchise. The timing could not have been more perfect for Disney. The pandemic brought them a captive audience. The entire world suddenly went on pause and an unprecedented number of people all of sudden found themselves at home, with nothing else to do but to stream on-demand videos. *The Mandalorian,* leveraging the widespread fan base of *Star Wars*, became one of the most popular TV series in 2020. In fact, according to one survey, *The Mandalorian* became 109 times more popular than the average TV series in the United States during this period.

In a typical *Star Wars* fashion, *The Mandalorian* was also followed by its own toy series. While Boba Fett (the Mandalorian himself) was already a popular action figure from days past, the series introduced a new character that proved to be an irresistible toy—The Child (AKA "Baby Yoda"). This toy became so much in demand that Amazon quickly sold out their entire inventory and had to put a stop on pre-orders. Even more so, they had to ask customers to request to be e-mailed when the toy becomes available again. Unsurprisingly, a whole new demand for vintage *Star Wars* toys also emerged. As people become reintroduced to the franchise, many felt the need to reconnect with their childhood memories and find the action figures that they used to own as children. In recent months, the price of some of these vintage toys increased significantly.

To understand better why some toys have the power to give us comfort and keep our imagination

176

How do we find comfort in unsettling times?

alive—long after we grow up—I spoke to Mark Boudreaux. Mark is a toy designer. In fact, he is one of the greatest toy designers in the world. He has worked as a designer of *Star Wars* toys since 1977, just as the franchise was first introduced. In recognition of his work, he was inducted in the *Pop Culture Hall of Fame* and the *Toy Collector's Hall of Fame*. In 2020, after 43 years designing *Star Wars* toys, Mark retired from Hasbro, the company that now owns the *Star Wars* toys franchise. Mark was also featured in the first episode of the hit Netflix series, *The Toys That Made Us*. The series opened with the story of the *Star Wars* toys—the most profitable toy franchise in history. But as they say at Hasbro, "All talk of toy sales aside, it"s nice to know people have something comforting like Baby Yoda to enjoy in these unsettling times."

Gjoko Muratovski: In 2020, you retired after 43 years of designing toys for the *Star Wars* universe. How did you become involved with this project?

Mark Boudreaux: I joined Kenner Toys in January 1977 while I was still a student at what is now the Ullman School of Design—I graduated the following year, in 1978. These kinds of industry placements are a typical part of the design education at the University of Cincinnati. The great thing about Kenner Toys was that it was a hometown company—they were right here in Cincinnati. When I got this job, I was their first co-op student in their newly formed

177

design department. Then, I realized that two other recent graduates from this school were already working in the same department—Jim Swearingen (Class of 1972) and Tom Osborne (Class of 1975). Tom was the Director of Design at Kenner and Jim was the Principle Conceptual Designer. Then, in February of that year—just a month or so after I joined Kenner—they acquired the *Star Wars* license from Lucasfilm. I was invited to work on this project from the very beginning. My first task was to design the Millennium Falcon. The rest is history, as they say. [Laughs]

Gjoko Muratovski: The origin story of the *Star Wars* toys franchise is quite interesting. In 1976, when George Lucas decided to commission toys to support the film that he was working on, he was turned down by all major toymakers, including Hasbro, who owns the franchise today. The only company that agreed to design and make the toys was Kenner. Jim Swearingen was the person who reviewed the script for the *Star Wars* film. Quite serendipitously, Jim was a sci-fi fan and he could immediately see that this film could translate into an exciting toy franchise. Jim took the trip to Lucasfilm in California to meet with George Lucas and discuss all of the details for the toy line. The most remarkable part of the deal was that Kenner kept 95 cents of each dollar made from the toys, while Lucasfilm and twentieth century Fox split a nickel. When *Star Wars* opened in the theaters in 1977, it quickly became the highest-grossing film of all time. Kenner made a fortune selling the toys.

When you first started working on *Star Wars*, did you have any idea of how successful this project would potentially become?

Mark Boudreaux: I'm not sure if anybody at the time could imagine how big this was going to be. I don't know if anybody knew the true potential of this franchise, with maybe the exception of Jim Swearingen. Jim read the *Star Wars* script when Kenner Toys were approached by Lucasfilm to design the toys for the film. He could straight away tell that there was something special about this story. He could just see the potential—the characters, the vehicles, the worlds that people could experience; everything was there. He realized that this would be something that was totally new; something that no one had ever seen before. He started the ball rolling and Kenner embraced his passion that the *Star Wars* project was something that the company should pursue.

Star Wars as a film franchise was certainly something that touched a nerve with everybody. Somehow everyone could relate to the story. And yes, it was "a long time ago, in a galaxy far, far away," but it was something that people could nevertheless connect with. George Lucas really did a great job telling a story that had something for everybody. There was the action, the good versus evil, there was some comedy, and there was a little bit of romance. All of these things are very relatable.

179

Now, 43 years later, *Star Wars* are still a part of our popular culture. You can see references from *Star Wars* all the time and everywhere. Whether they are from the classic films or the new *Mandalorian* show, *Star Wars* references are just omnipresent. And there is certainly a lot of passion involved. There is also a very large community of people that call themselves *Star Wars* fans. And it's really this community that makes *Star Wars* the success that they are. It's really all about the fans. We can make toys all day, but it's the fans that we're making this product for. It's their passion that feeds our passion. The true toy fans and collectors are as passionate as the toy designers are. For them— and for us—every detail counts. We put an incredible attention to the detail of every toy that we design; especially to those toys that we design for the older fans of the franchise, the collectors.

Gjoko Muratovski: Why do you think the *Star Wars* toys became so successful?

Mark Boudreaux: You know, when the first films came out, there was nothing else like it. People were lining up around the planet to go and see *Star Wars*. And back then, *Star Wars* films would stay at the theaters for a year. Even the best films today only stay at the theaters for maybe three or four weeks. *Star Wars* stayed around for quite a while. But you also need to understand the context of the time. Back then we didn't have social media, we didn't have computers, and we didn't have so many things to distract us. So

How do we find comfort in unsettling times?

Star Wars really was something that you would go and see multiple times. "Hey, let's go see *Star Wars* again," people would say. And the following just grew and grew and grew. And with time, this following became a community. The toys were an extension of the films. The toys would allow you to recreate the excitement from the films at home. For fans that grew up with these films and these toys—fans that were young at the time—this was an experience that they have never forgotten.

In the meantime, they got older and they started having kids of their own, but their connection with *Star Wars* is still there. Kenner, which is now part of Hasbro, is still producing the same *Star Wars* toys that these people had as children. They see them, and they remember what it was like to be a kid back in the day. They probably no longer have these toys, but they would really like to have them again. They would like to rekindle their childhood memories. They allow themselves to be children again. And they would like to share that experience with their children as well. Toys like this have the ability to create exceptionally strong bonds with people.

Toys are often an integral part of the childhood memories that we all have. A lot of the older *Star Wars* fans are now passing along these toys and their memories to their kids, and their kids will be passing these along to theirs. They are timeless and multi-generational and, in this regard, many fans consider their *Star Wars* toys to be heirlooms.

Design in the Age of Change

Gjoko Muratovski: This is one of the most successful toy series in history. According to the Netflix *Star Wars* episode on *The Toys That Made Us*, between 1978 and 2020, there have been over one billion *Star Wars* toys sold. As they pointed out, if you melt down all these toys, you will have enough plastic to make one colossal toy figure that would dwarf the Empire State Building.

Mark Boudreaux: Oh, my goodness. [Laughs] That's one heck of a number. I knew it was quite high, but I didn't know it was quite that high. That's a lot of toys.

Gjoko Muratovski: Yes, that's a lot. According to Netflix, the *Star Wars* film franchise to date has grossed $7 billion, but the *Star Wars* toys have grossed $14 billion–twice the amount that the films have made. That's pretty incredible, Mark.

Mark Boudreaux: I feel so fortunate that I have had the opportunity to play a small role in such a big story.

Gjoko Muratovski: So, what are your favorite *Star Wars* toys?

Mark Boudreaux: That's a big question. You know, there were a lot of exciting things I was able to work on with *Star Wars* over the years. However, I've always been kind of "the vehicle guy." I've worked on action figures, as well, but vehicles were always what I had a passion for. Kenner and Hasbro allowed me to pursue my passion in this area. But if I have to pick my favorite toy, I would say that the Millennium Falcon is nearer and dearer to me. Over the years, I've had the privilege of working on all major Millennium Falcon versions.

I have other favorite toys as well. You know, the action figure for Boba Fett, the Mandalorian bounty hunter, is a big favorite of mine. Jim Swearingen designed this toy. As you know, this became one of the most notorious action figures from the original collection of 1978. In the world of *Star Wars*, the original Boba Fett figure is known as the "Holy Grail." This is the most renowned single *Star Wars* toy item and, at the time, this character was not even featured in the film. This toy could not be purchased at any stores and was only available via special mail-in promotion. Originally, Boba Fett was advertised with a rocket-firing capability in his backpack. However, due to safety concerns, the rocket-firing feature was never available to the public. Recently, a leaked prototype of the rocket-firing Boba Fett fetched $225,000 at an eBay auction.

People today are so much into *The Mandalorian* series. I was so excited to see Boba Fett return. He was too cool of a character to just die in the *Return of the Jedi* installment. So, to have him return with his own series, and have him fly around in the Slave I spaceship—which is another vehicle that I designed—is really cool.

Gjoko Muratovski: I am surprised that you didn't mention Baby Yoda here.

Design in the Age of Change

Mark Boudreaux: Yes, Baby Yoda! Well, now we also know his name, which was not disclosed when the character was introduced—it's Grogu. That is a very interesting character and there is a very interesting story behind it. We knew that *The Mandalorian* was coming out, and Lucasfilm has shared many details with us in advance of the series so that we can start developing toys prior to the show release, but Baby Yoda was kept a secret even from us. This was a character that was really important to Mr Lucas and he really wanted to keep him "under wraps." We were informed about the character in general, but we were not given any specific detail about how he looks. As per Mr Lucas' request, we were asked not to work on the development of this toy until the character gets revealed on the show. He wanted the character to be a surprise. Once we got the green light to work on this, Hasbro quickly put together a "strike team"—a small task force made of designers, sculptors, engineers, packaging specialists, etc.—to develop this product in a record fashion. We developed multiple versions of this product that are now on the market. The little guy was so adorable that everybody wanted him so badly and they wanted him right now.

Gjoko Muratovski: What is your design process, Mark?

Mark Boudreaux: The design process for me starts with knowing the story. Let's take *Star Wars*

as an example. Whether you do an action figure or a spacecraft, you first need to understand
what that character or vehicle is all about. What's
its purpose in the story? How does it relate from
one aspect to another? Is the vehicle important to
a particular figure? Is it important to the story
point?

Being able to understand the story is probably the
most important aspect of the process. Because once
you understand the story you can start to dig deeper
into what the design needs to project and what's the
appropriate scale. Then, you need to think about your
stakeholders. What's the appropriate audience? Is this
being designed for a young fan? Is it being designed for a
collector?

All of these things that you need to consider form
a checklist of things that you must take into account
as you design. For example, for collectors, the dec-
oration and the amount of detail that you put on to
an item are very important. You will approach your
design for collectors differently than if you design for
young children. Younger audiences would be more
attracted to cleaner versions with more vibrant colors.
Whereas, if you design for collectors, the designs are
going to look more authentic and "battle worn." High-
end collector items will feature much more compli-
cated detailing than toys that children will actually
play with.

Then, in the initial stage of the design process, I just
like to take a blank piece of paper and a pen, and I'll just
start drawing the concept. Once I get it the way I like, I'll

scan it, and then I'll start to manipulate it digitally.
I guess that's a little bit "old school," but that's how I do
it. A lot of the younger designers that we have on our
team will probably just start drawing right on the computer. I like a nice mix between digital technologies
and pen and paper. Digital can let you do some things
that you can't really do just with a pen and a piece of
paper. But both can complement each other in a really
great way.

Gjoko Muratovski: What would you say was the most
exciting part about working on this franchise?

Mark Boudreaux: The most exciting thing for me was
that I could expand the *Star Wars* universe beyond
what George Lucas initially envisioned. I was allowed
to design characters and vehicles that were never
depicted in the original films, and my designs became
as much a part of the *Star Wars* universe as those that
you could see featured on the screen. Mr Lucas loved
this work.

Gjoko Muratovski: Mark, thank you so much for
being my guest. I love how you still have so much passion for *Star Wars* after working on this project for
43 years.

Mark Boudreaux: Thank you for having me, Gjoko.
Working on the *Star Wars* project has really been
an once-in-a-lifetime experience for me. After all
these years, I still feel proud to have designed

How do we find comfort in unsettling times?

products that have touched so many peoples' lives in
so many ways.

May the Force be with you, and with all the *Star Wars*
fans.

Survival by design
Afterword by
Ken Friedman

Design in the Age of Change documents a quiet revolution in the practice of design. With ten carefully selected conversations, this book represents some of the most prominent design figures at work in a profession that is extraordinarily visible. The collective work of these ten individuals touches the lives of billions of people, yet their efforts are often invisible. While everyone is aware that we live in a world that is designed for us, very few know about the people behind the designs, and even less about the ideas and the principles that guide their work. We are experiencing a time of extraordinary change. New ideas are emerging while old and established conventions are under challenge. As the world is changing, the field of design is adapting.

Four issues came to my mind repeatedly in reading these ten conversations.

Humanity has experienced such times before. Every generation believes that the changes it must address are extraordinary and unprecedented. So it must have seemed to the human beings who settled the first cities at the time of the agricultural revolution. So it appeared when such innovations as cuneiform, hieroglyphics, and the alphabet enabled us to record our words and share them at a distance and across time. That particular revolution took on force again when printing was born in China, and yet again when the Gutenberg press helped to change the cultural world of Europe. The world hasn't had one industrial revolution, but several. The first of these took place over two million years ago when our pre-human ancestors carved and chipped the first stone tools. We've seen other industrial revolutions in the years since, and each of these revolutions has been remarkable in the way that it brought into being a new sense of the normal.

It is equally remarkable to realize that each successive iteration of new times soon faded into the background of human experience as daily life.

When I was young, people might have worried when they saw someone walk down a busy street alone talking out loud with someone who wasn't there. When we walk down a city street today, it often seems that the majority of our fellow pedestrians are talking with people who aren't there. In a few short years, this behavior has changed from a mental health concern to a thread in the fabric of urban life.

A fascinating literature traces the growth and development of these successive revolutions. Books such as Carolyn Marvin's *When Old Technologies Were New*, Jean Gimpel's *The Medieval Machine*, or Patrice Flichy's *Dynamics of Modern Communication* document historical times when the past reached for the future. A few years from now, someone will read *Design in the Age of Change* to understand how people designed the artifacts and inventions that are changing our lives now much as the moldboard plow and the wind-powered mill changed life in the past.

No single invention, no one development changes everything—but together, the products and services that emerge through human design agency combine to bring about a new era.

The second fact that strikes me in reading these conversations is that we face an existential threat to human life on our planet unlike any past event in recorded history. The closest comparisons are extinction-level events that changed the course of life on earth. In a powerful book, Elizabeth Kolbert describes this as *The Sixth Extinction*. The increasing likelihood of this extinction-level event emerges in response to the catastrophic climate change for which human civilization is responsible.

The problems now on our horizon are likely to change our world in ferocious ways. We see the effects of the change across a range of problems—and each problem cascades into the next. Take the likely impact of catastrophic climate change on one problem alone: refugees.

We need only compare the problem of climate refugees with recent crises to see the scale and scope of what we face.

The world barely managed to cope with the impact of 6,600,000 refugees seeking shelter in the wake of the conflict in Syria. This created problems across the Middle East. It also led to problems in Europe with roughly 1,000,000 Syrian refugees. The effects have been immense for the immigration and social support systems of the European nations that welcomed refugees. These had follow-on effects for finances and taxes, leading, in turn, to political change.

Catastrophic climate change is likely to see hundreds of millions of refugees who struggle to flee one part of the world for another. As much of a disaster as six million refugees seemed to be—with as many people again displaced inside Syria—this number is small compared to the likely displacement of climate refugees.

A 2017 study by Charles Geisler and Ben Currens used then-current projections from the Intergovernmental Panel on Climate Change (IPCC) to predict the likely impact of rising sea levels on the low-elevation coastal zone. In 2000, roughly 630,000,000 people lived in low-elevation coastal zones threatened by rising sea levels. Most of these people are at risk of displacement. Current estimates suggest population growth in this zone to 1,400,000,000 (1.4 billion) people by 2060. With oceans rising further by the end of the century, Geisler extrapolates the number of possible climate refugees to as many as two billion people by 2100; one-fifth of the human population. According to Geisler:

> The colliding forces of human fertility, submerging coastal zones, residential retreat, and impediments to inland resettlement is a huge problem. We offer preliminary estimates of the lands unlikely to support new waves of climate refugees due to the residues of war, exhausted natural resources, declining net primary productivity, desertification, urban sprawl, land concentration, "paving

the planet" with roads, and greenhouse gas storage zones offsetting permafrost melt.

(cited in Friedlander 2017: n.pag.)

There is simply no enlightened way to deal with the consequences of a crisis on this scale. In the wake of the refugee problems created by the Syrian Civil War, several populations turned angry, electing right-wing nationalist and populist governments. It is difficult to comprehend the turmoil that will come with 300 times as many refugees.

The only way to avoid this kind of disaster is effective action to reduce anthropogenic climate change. This is unlikely to happen on the time scale required if we are to prevent hundreds of millions of deaths. The social, economic, and human disruptions that we will face are likely to deform and reshape civilizations. We can barely understand problems of this size in emotional terms.

Stephen Emmott's book *Ten Billion* explains what is coming. Public health policy researcher, Kate Saffin, summarized Emmott's conclusions in a book review:

[Emmott] rather (obviously) proposes that the options to improve use of resources—and therefore to accommodate the population increase—are to either develop technology or instigate radical behaviour changes. He doesn't think that either will work out, because the technologies aren't being developed properly and because behaviour change at such a scale would need the help of governments and he rightly doesn't see any evidence that that will happen. He reminds us of the various UN committees charged with protecting the planet, to little effect, and of

the international summits that fail to secure meaningful pledges and commitments. Emmott also discusses the charge of consumerism and the nature of corporations built for unending growth as crucial parts of the problem, and it is really his despondency that politicians are unwilling to seem unpopular and that a "radical transformation of corporate culture" is very unlikely to happen that leads him to one of his final sentences: "I think we're f*cked."
(Saffin 2013: n.pag.)

A couple years back, I wrote an editorial in the journal *She Ji* to summarize the situation. In it, I discuss Jørgen Randers's report to the Norwegian Parliament and the public referendum on Randers's actionable and reasonably costed proposals to mitigate catastrophic climate change in a nation long noted for environmental awareness. The politicians and the public voted against the proposals. Randers, a co-author of the Club of Rome report *Limits to Growth*, reached a sad conclusion. Rather than act on climate change, he said, "People would rather go shopping."

In a *New York Times* article, Nathaniel Rich explains why—despite all that we know—we are not likely to avert the coming catastrophe. Rich interviewed John Sununu, chief of staff to President George H.W. Bush. Sununu helped to prevent the United States from signing an enforceable climate treaty in the early 1990s. When Rich asked him why, Sununu explained it—and he explains why political leaders take the same positions today:

[The] leaders in the world at that time were at a stage where they were all looking how to seem like they were

194

supporting the [climate] policy without having to make
hard commitments that would cost their nations serious
resources ... Frankly that's about where we are today.

(cited in Rich 2018: n.pag.)

With little likelihood of change, we will face global disruptions far larger than the problems that led to the Russian
Revolution, the collapse of the Weimar Republic, the Black
Death, or the earlier disruptions that led to the collapse of
the Roman Empire. This, too, is the new era of change.

The third fact of our time as it appears from within
the world of design is more hopeful. Designers today
struggle as never before to deal responsibly with the
impact of their work on the world in which we live.

Not so long ago, designers began to recognize that
their work had adverse effects. Victor Papanek offered a
forthright assessment:

There are professions more harmful than industrial
design, but only a very few of them. And possibly only
one profession is phonier. Advertising design, in persuading people to buy things they don't need, with money
they don't have, in order to impress others who don't
care, is probably the phoniest field in existence today.
Industrial design, by concocting the tawdry idiocies
hawked by advertisers, comes a close second.

(Papanek 1997: ix)

Today, many designers give thought to how they can
mitigate or even avoid the harms in which the design profession plays a role. This is difficult, but as difficult as it

is, this challenge is on the agenda for many of the world's designers.

The fourth and perhaps the most hopeful aspect of this moment is the way in which human beings are reconceiving our world. This is a concept that philosopher Arturo Escobar describes as the pluriverse—a world in which each of us has an equal share, each of us has equal rights, and each of us has the right to address the world from a responsible position within our own culture and world view. One aspect of this view is an understanding of how it is that we as human beings are part of a world larger than ourselves; responsible for our actions within that world; and accountable for the influence we exert on the world around us.

Will we be able to forge a different path to the future? There is no way to know. The evidence to date is not hopeful. Even so, the question is at the front of mind for many designers today.

Eleven design leaders came together to share their ideas in thoughtful conversation: Carole Bilson, Karim Rashid, Natalie Nixon, Bruce Mau, Steven Heller, Alok Vaid-Menon, Randall Wilson, Don Norman, Ida Telalbasic, Mark Boudreaux, each of them talking with Gjoko Muratovski.

It is a privilege to learn from them.

References

Emmott, Stephen (2013), *Ten Billion*, New York: Vintage Books.

Escobar, Arturo (2018), *Designs for the Pluriverse: Radical Interdependence, Autonomy, and the Making of Worlds*, Durham: Duke University Press.

Flichy, Patrice (1995), *Dynamics of Modern Communication: The Shaping and Impact of New Communication Technologies*, London: SAGE Publications.

Friedlander, Blaine (2017), "Rising seas could result in 2 billion refugees by 2100," Cornell Chronicle, June 19, https://news.cornell.edu/stories/2017/06/rising-seas-could-result-2-billion-refugees-2100. Accessed November 16, 2021.

Friedman, Ken (2018), "The Earth will be here. Will we?" *She Ji: The Journal of Design, Economics, and Innovation*, 4:3, Autumn, pp. 203–08, https://doi.org/10.1016/j.sheji.2018.07.002. Accessed November 16, 2021.

Geisler, Charles and Ben, Currens (2017), "Impediments to inland resettlement under conditions of accelerated sea level rise," *Land Use Policy*, 66, July, pp. 322–30, http://dx.doi.org/10.1016/j.landusepol.2017.03.029. Accessed November 16, 2021.

Gimpel, Jean (1992), *The Medieval Machine: The Industrial Revolution of the Middle Ages*, London: Pimlico Press.

Kolbert, Elizabeth (2014), *The Sixth Extinction: An Unnatural History*, New York: Henry Holt and Company.

Marvin, Carolyn (1988), *When Old Technologies Were New: Thinking About Electric Communication in the Late Nineteenth Century*, Oxford: Oxford University Press.

Papanek, Victor (1997), *Design for the Real World*, 2nd ed, London: Thames and Hudson.

Rich, Nathaniel (2018), "Losing Earth: The decade we almost stopped climate change," *The New York Times Magazine*, August 1, https://www.nytimes.com/interactive/2018/08/01/magazine/climate-change-losingearth.html. Accessed August 14, 2018.

Saffin, Kate (2013), "Book review: 10 billion by Stephen Emmott," *London School of Economics Book Blog*, https://blogs.lse.ac.uk/lsereviewofbooks/2013/11/19/book-review-10-billion/. Accessed November 16, 2021.

Contributors

Author

Gjoko Muratovski is an award-winning designer and innovation consultant working with a wide range of universities, Fortune 500 companies, and various governments from around the world. Throughout his career he has held numerous leadership and high-profile appointments at various academic and professional institutions. He served as a member of many thought-leading organizations such as the Forbes Councils, Stanford Institute for Innovation in Developing Economies, Oxford Digital Leaders Network, and the Yale Higher Education Leadership Summit. Muratovski also served as an Endowed Chair and Director of The Myron E. Ullman, Jr School of Design between 2016 and 2021, and led the school through a transformative period of change. Originally founded in 1869, the Ullman School of Design at the University of Cincinnati is the oldest public design school in the United States.

Contributors

Srini R. Srinivasan is the President of the World Design Organization (WDO). Originally founded in 1957, the WDO is a global design organization that holds a special United Nations (UN) consultative status. In this role, Srinivasan works with various UN agencies, foundations, city governments, and WDO members from across the globe, on developing design programs aimed at creating positive global impact. He is also the Chairman and CEO of Lumium Design, an award-winning product design consultancy with offices in the United States, India, and Japan.

Carole Bilson is the President of the Design Management Institute (DMI). In this capacity, she represents a community of 30,000 design leaders from more than 60 countries. Prior to this role, she was the first African American woman to become head of global design and user experience at a major corporation, where her team received 49 patents and twelve international design awards. She was also the worldwide product line manager for the Kodak Picturemaker™—a product that has earned the company over a billion dollars.

Karim Rashid is one of the most prolific and most recognizable designers of our time. With over 4000 designs in production, more than 300 awards to his name, and clients that span across 40 countries—Karim is a design icon. *TIME* magazine once called him "The Most Famous Industrial Designer in All the Americas." His works are in the permanent collections of the Museum of Modern Art (MoMA) in New York and in San Francisco, the Cooper Hewitt Smithsonian Design Museum, and the British Design Museum. Earlier this year, Karim received the highest and most prestigious design award in the United States—the 2020 American Prize for Design by the Chicago Athenaeum. This highly coveted award is given to outstanding individuals for their lifetime achievements in the field of design.

Natalie Nixon is an African American design thinker, creativity strategist, and a Fellow of the London-based Royal Society of Arts. She is also a contributor to *Inc. Magazine* and a member of the Forbes Councils. Natalie incorporates her background in anthropology, foresight, fashion, and design management, as well as her cross-cultural experiences living and working in the United States, Brazil, Israel, Germany, United Kingdom, Portugal, and Sri Lanka to inform her approach to creativity. She is the award-winning author of the book *The Creativity Leap*—one of the Top 40 business books of 2020.

Bruce Mau is an eminent Canadian designer, innovator, and educator. His design work transcends disciplines and categories. Mau had a stellar career over the last several decades, and he is a household name in the fields of design and architecture. In addition to his many awards and accolades, he is also named as an Honorary Royal Designer for Industry by the Royal Society of Arts. His books *S,M,L,XL* (with Rem Koolhaas), *Life Style*, *Massive Change*, and *MC24: Bruce Mau's 24 Principles for Designing Massive Change in your Life and Work* are widely read and have received both cult status and critical acclaim.

Steven Heller is a celebrated author, editor, and design critic. As of now, Heller has published close to 200 books on design, and contributed to hundreds of other design publications, with more coming. As a design critic, he has documented and reflected on the history and practice of graphic design with incredible depth, breadth, and scope. For more than 30 years he was an Art Director for *The New York Times* and writer for *The New York Times Book Review*. Heller is also the recipient of several highly prestigious awards, including the AIGA's Medal for Lifetime Achievement Award, the Art Directors Club Hall of Fame Award, and the National Design Award, which was presented to him at a White House ceremony by the First Lady of the United States at the time, Michelle Obama.

Alok Vaid-Menon is a highly prominent figure of the gender non-conforming movement. They are a gender non-conforming activist, writer, poet, fashion designer, and performance artist, widely recognized for their distinctive style. As a mixed-media artist, Vaid-Menon explores themes of gender, race, trauma, belonging, and the human condition. They are a very passionate advocate for issues related to gender neutrality, degendering fashion, and the challenges that the trans and gender non-conforming communities face on a daily basis. Vaid-Menon is frequently covered by the press and the media—from the PBS News Hour and MTV to *The New Yorker*, *Vogue*, and the HBO documentary, *The Trans List*.

Randall Wilson is an African American fashion design illustrator, education, and the Coordinator for Diversity and Inclusion at the Ullman School of Design. Over the years, in addition to maintain his interest in fashion, Wilson, also worked with numerous social service support programs. He taught special needs students at a local Cincinnati high school, he assisted HIV/AIDS patients with their daily tasks and distribution of their medicine, he provided assisted living services to people with mental disabilities, he served as a rehabilitation manager for criminal offenders, and he even worked as a probation officer for the Adult Parole Authority.

Don Norman is the former Vice President for Advanced Technology at Apple and for the past five years he served as the Director of the Design Lab at the University of California San Diego (UCSD). Norman is widely recognized as the ultimate authority on all matters related to user experience and human-centric design. He is best known for his books on design, especially *The Design of Everyday Things* and *Emotional Design*. He is also the co-founder of the new global initiative, the Future of Design Education.

Ida Telalbasic is a service design strategist with expert knowledge in alternative economies, complementary currencies, and entrepreneurial ecosystems. Telalbasic also brings a unique global perspective to her work. She was born in Bosnia, grew up in Zimbabwe, studied in Italy, and now lives and works in the United Kingdom. Currently, she is teaching at Loughborough University London, Imperial College London, Central Saint Martins, and the University of Oxford.

Design in the Age of Change

Mark Boudreaux is one of the lead designers behind the *Star Wars* toys collection. He has worked on the *Star Wars* toys since 1977, just as the franchise was first introduced. In recognition of his work, he was inducted in the Pop Culture Hall of Fame and the Toy Collector's Hall of Fame. In 2020, after 43 years designing *Star Wars* toys, Mark retired from Hasbro—one of the world's largest toys and entertainment companies.

Ken Friedman is one of the most notable design scholars in the world. Friedman is a Foreign High-End Expert and Chair Professor of Design Innovation Studies at the Tongji University College of Design and Innovation in Shanghai, China, and a Visiting Professor at Lund University in Sweden. Friedman is also the founding Editor-in-Chief of 设计 *She Ji: The Journal of Design, Economics, and Innovation*, published by Tongji University Press in collaboration with Elsevier.